LEFT-HANDED GUITAR
THE COMPLETE METHOD

by
Troy Stetina

ISBN 978-0-7935-8788-9

HAL•LEONARD®
CORPORATION
7777 W. BLUEMOUND RD. P.O. BOX 13819 MILWAUKEE, WI 53213

Visit Hal Leonard Online at
www.halleonard.com

CONTENTS

Welcome to Left-Handed Guitar!

As you are undoubtedly already aware, society's preference for right-handedness runs deep. And nowhere has this been more true than in the field of guitar. In years past, left-handed players have had to adapt their technique to right-handed guitars, playing them upside down and "backwards." Thankfully, that is changing. Many guitar companies today routinely make left-handed versions.

Guitar methods and magazines have also had a strong right-handed bias—so much so that the fretting hand is commonly called "the left hand" and the picking hand is called "the right hand." More significantly, however, the chord and neck diagrams are always shown from the right-handed perspective, and this is likely to remain standard practice.

This guitar method is different. It gets you started with a wide cross-section of the basic guitar techniques and styles—all from a left-handed player's perspective. And at the end of the method, it offers tips for using the various right-hand information you'll find in other books and methods. Good luck…and enjoy!

What you'll learn

This book is arranged in sections. Each focuses on learning a different set of musical "tools" and applying that information to the appropriate styles of guitar. The sections are arranged in a logical, progressive sequence. They include:

- **Reading standard musical notation**. This section teaches a number of well-known *classical* and *folk* melodies as well as a few *rock* riffs as it acquaints you with the basics of reading music.

- **Chord boxes and strumming notation**. This section covers common strumming patterns and chord progressions seen in the vocal accompaniment styles of *rock, folk,* and *country* guitar.

- **Reading tablature**. This section covers single-note, *boogie*-style, early rock 'n' roll rhythm figures as well as single-note *modern rock* riffs and arpeggiation.

- **Power chords**. This section includes chordal riffs and techniques common in *hard rock* and *metal* guitar styles, including hammer-ons, pull-offs, and palm muting.

- **Barre chords**. Here, chord progressions of various styles are played using full, movable major, minor, and seventh barre chords.

- **The blues**. This section deals with elements common to the *blues* idiom, from basic blues to *blues-rock* and *Texas blues*.

- **Fingerstyle guitar**. This section shows basic fingerstyle technique in a variety of styles, including *pop, folk, ragtime, country, rockabilly,* and *classical*.

Finally, in-depth chord and scale reference sections complete the method, offering intermediate to advanced-level information that you can study at your own pace.

Famous Lefties

One could argue quite convincingly that lefties have played a disproportionately large role in the evolution of modern guitar playing.

Probably the most well-known guitar hero of the "sinister" persuasion (*sinister* literally means "of the left hand") was **Jimi Hendrix**. Hendrix brought a new level of virtuosic performance to the rock genre in the 1960s. His unique fuzz tone, blues mastery, and out-of-this-world psychedelic outings inspired and influenced a whole generation of guitarists and helped to redefine rock music. He played a right-handed Fender Stratocaster guitar upside-down and re-strung in reverse.

Another prominent lefty, who came on the scene in the early 1970s, was **Tony Iommi**, guitarist for the English metal band Black Sabbath. Iommi defined the heavy metal sound of the seventies with his dark, thickly distorted tone. Many successful metal guitarists today credit Black Sabbath with being among their major influences. Tony favored Gibson SG models.

More recently, left-handed grunge revolutionary **Kurt Cobain** turned the world of popular music upside down as guitarist and vocalist for Nirvana. Cobain led the Seatle-based grunge movement of the early 1990s until his untimely death in 1994. He played a left-handed Fender Jagstang guitar.

A list of other significant lefties would have to include blues legend **Albert King**. He so favored the upper portion of second pentatonic "box" shape that it is sometimes referred to as the "Albert King box." King played without restringing the guitar, thus leaving the strings "upside down" from their normal sequence (that is, the lowest sounding string was nearest the floor). Although not principally a guitarist, **Paul McCartney** is/was another trend-setting lefty. The former Beatles bassist has clearly had an enormous impact upon popular music. Other great lefties include blues giant **Otis Rush**, surf-guitar pioneer **Dick Dale**, guitarist **Al McKay** of Earth, Wind, and Fire, fusion virtuoso **Carlos Rio**, and blues-rock contemporary **Doyle Bramhall**.

Playing Left-Handed Guitar Today

In the past, left-handed players had to "invert" right-handed guitars, playing them upside-down and backwards. In order that the strings remained in their standard order (with the highest-sounding string nearest the floor) the guitar had to be restrung in reverse, which required reversing both the nut and bridge saddles as well, since they are designed to accomodate the particular thicknesses of the various strings.

Today, however, guitar manufacturers routinely make left-handed versions of their models, although they must generally be custom-ordered. The left-handed guitars shown below are simply mirror-image duplicates of their standard right-handed counterparts.

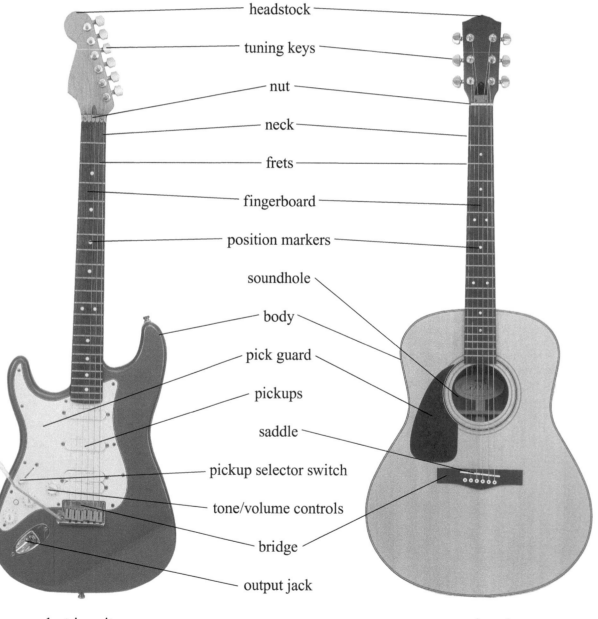

headstock

tuning keys

nut

neck

frets

fingerboard

position markers

soundhole

body

pick guard

pickups

saddle

pickup selector switch

tone/volume controls

bridge

output jack

electric guitar

acoustic guitar

Tuning

Tuning the guitar essentially means correcting the pitches of the open strings. This is accomplished by adjusting the tuning keys on the headstock of the guitar, thereby tightening or loosening the tension of each string appropriately. The tighter the string, the higher the pitch. There are several different methods of tuning.

Using a piano

If you have access to a piano or keyboard, you can play each of the notes shown below and tune the corresponding string on the guitar. Tighten slowly, and be careful not to overtighten.

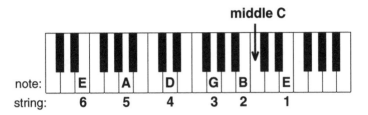

Electronic tuner

An electronic guitar tuner simplifies the tuning process by "listening" to the pitch and displaying whether the string is sharp (too high), flat (too low), or in tune.

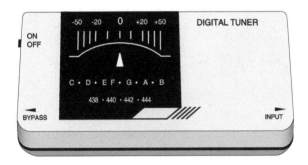

Relative tuning

Tuning the strings to each other by ear is called *relative tuning*. This is done in the following manner:

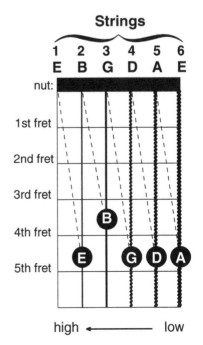

- Assuming the lowest-sounding string (string 6) is correctly tuned to E, press it down behind the fifth fret, then play that note together with the open string 5. Adjust the pitch of string 5 until it matches that of string 6.

- Press down on string 5 behind the fifth fret, and tune the open string 4 to it.

- Press down on string 4 behind the fifth fret, and tune the open string 3 to it.

- Press down on string 3 behind the fourth fret, and tune the open string 2 to it.

- Press down on string 2 behind the fifth fret, and tune the open string 2 to it.

A Few More Things

There are just a few more details to think about before we get started...

Sitting vs. standing

Sitting is probably the most comfortable and least tiring method for practicing guitar. The guitar should rest on your left leg, balancing its weight evenly so that you can hold it in place without pressure from either hand. Notice the slight upward tilt of the neck.

Sitting

Standing

Eventually, you can play standing up as well. For now, however, it's probably best to put that extra effort to better use—playing.

The left and right hands

Hold the neck of the guitar with your *right hand*, with the thumb resting comfortably behind the neck. Hold the pick with your *left hand*, between your thumb and index finger. You don't need to grip the neck or the pick too tightly—just firm enough to hold on.

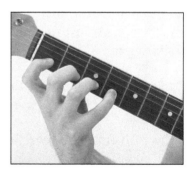

Right hand position (fingers)

Right hand position (thumb)

Left hand position (with pick)

Fingerboard grids

Fingerboard grids, or diagrams, represent a portion of the fretboard and show you graphically where to play the notes. Circles are drawn onto the diagram to indicate where to place your finger. To play a note, you press down on the appropriate string, right behind the appropriate fret, with one of your right-hand fingers. Then pick that string with your left hand to sound the note.

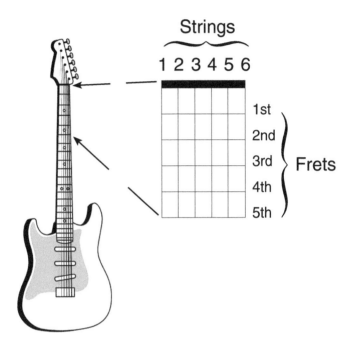

Your right-hand fingers are numbered 1 through 4, starting with your index finger.

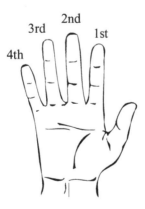

Reading Music on the Staff

Music is a language with its own symbols, structures, rules, and even exceptions to those rules. To become a proficient guitarist, it is best to become familiar with the symbols used to notate music. While it is true that extensive note-reading ability is not required in order to create or perform music in many styles—rock, pop, blues, metal, etc.—the fact remains that a basic understanding of standard music notation is generally helpful. And in some styles—for example, classical guitar and jazz—it is indispensible. So we will begin this method with a short section on reading the notes in "open position."

Notes

Like the two different sides of a coin, notes have two distinct aspects to them. They have a **pitch** ("highness" or "lowness"), which is indicated by the note's position on the staff, and they have a **rhythmic value**, indicating how long that pitch lasts. Here are the most basic rhythmic values:

Whole note	Half note	Quarter note
o	𝅗𝅥	𝅘𝅥
4 beats	2 beats	1 beat

The rhythmic value, or length of a note, is always given in terms of "beats." The **beat** is simply the underlying pulse that we all instinctively sense in music when we tap our foot or dance. A quarter note is the simplest rhythm: one beat per note. Half notes are two beats each, and whole notes are four beats each. It's just like fractions—two quarters equal a half, and two halves equal a whole.

The staff

Notes are positioned on the **staff**, which consists of five parallel, horizontal lines and the four spaces in between those lines. Each line and space represents a different pitch. Higher-sounding pitches appear higher on the staff, lower-sounding pitches appear lower.

When notes rise above the top of the staff or go below the bottom, **ledger lines** are used to extend the staff.

The treble clef

A symbol called a **clef** indicates the position of the specific note names on the staff. Different clefs are used in music for different ranges of instruments. Guitar notation is written using a **treble clef**:

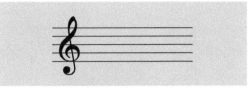

A treble clef is actually a very fancy-looking letter "G," which wraps around and ends, centering on the second line from the bottom. This means that line has the pitch with the letter name G. The other lines and spaces continue the alphabet from there, using only the letter names A through G, then repeating. The letter names of the lines and spaces are:

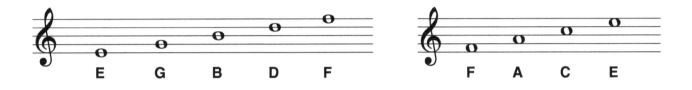

E   G   B   D   F   F   A   C   E

An easy way to remember the names of the lines is "Every Good Band Draws Fans." For the spaces, remember the word "**face**."

Measures and time signatures

To keep track of time, notes are divided into **measures**, or **bars**. Bar lines separate each measure and a heavy double bar indicates the ending of a piece of music. A **time signature**, or **meter**, tells you how many beats will appear in each measure (top number) and what kind of note gets one beat (bottom number).

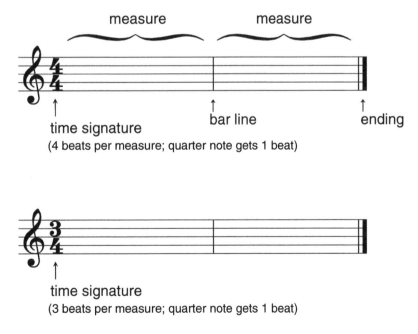

measure   measure

time signature   bar line   ending
(4 beats per measure; quarter note gets 1 beat)

time signature
(3 beats per measure; quarter note gets 1 beat)

String 1: E

The following photos and diagrams show how to play the first three notes on the high E string. Underneath, these notes are shown as they appear on the staff.

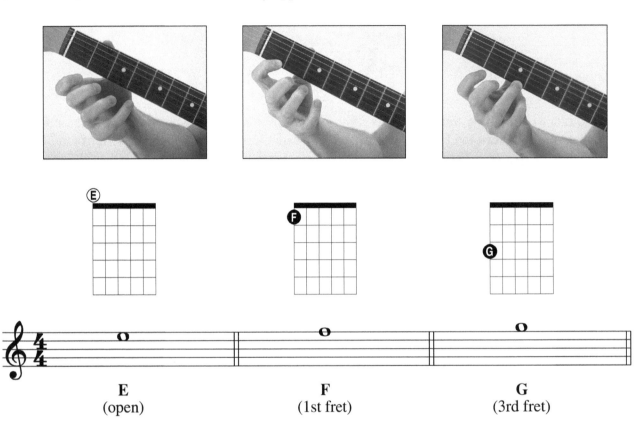

The following examples use only these three notes E, F, and G. The beat, or count, is written below the first line to help you with the timing.

E–F–G

First Song

String 2: B

The following photos and diagrams show how to play the first three notes on the B string.

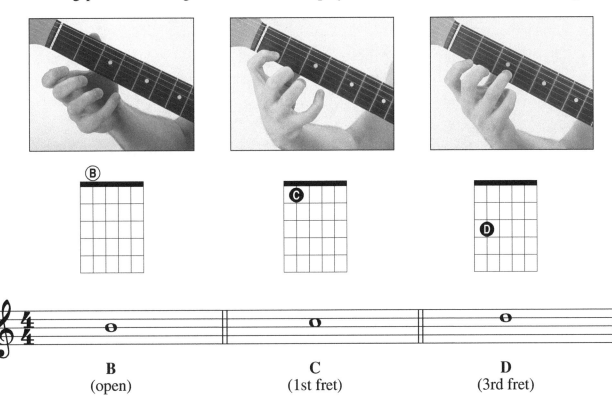

B
(open)

C
(1st fret)

D
(3rd fret)

The example below uses notes on the B string.

B–C–D

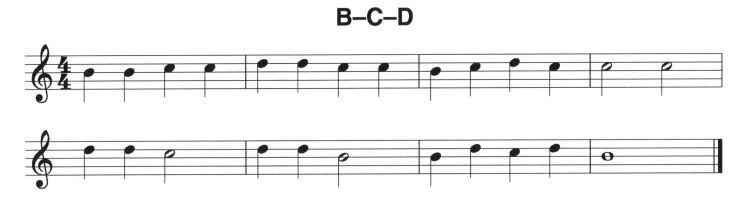

This classical melody uses notes on both the E and B strings. (By the way, Ludwig van Beethoven—the composer of the symphony from which this is drawn—was left-handed.)

Ode to Joy

Rests and Dotted Half Notes

A **rest** is a space of silence, or a pause. Rests are just like notes in that they have their own rhythmic values, which tell you exactly how long you need to hold the strings quiet.

The line below uses all three types of rests.

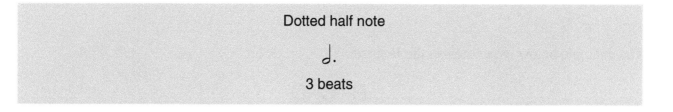

A dot placed after a half note extends its length to three beats, instead of the usual two.

Dotted half note

♩.

3 beats

The tune below uses rests as well as dotted half notes.

When the Saints Go Marching In

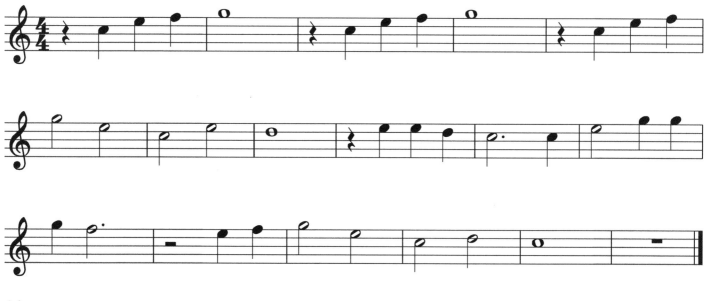

Sharps

The frets that lie in between the notes we have learned are named using **sharps** and/or **flats**. A sharp sign (♯) raises the pitch of a note one fret, and a flat sign (♭) lowers a note one fret. Here, we will look at several sharps.

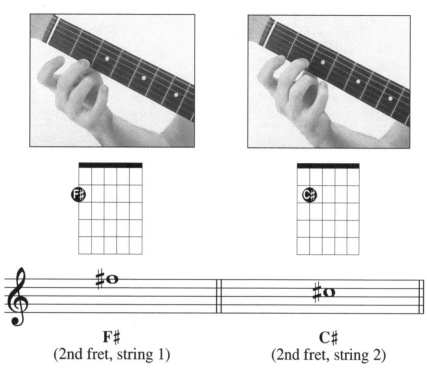

F♯
(2nd fret, string 1)

C♯
(2nd fret, string 2)

Practice playing F♯ and C♯ in the exercise below.

F♯ and C♯

A natural sign (♮) cancels a previous sharp, indicating that you should play the note "un-sharped."

Secret Agent Groove

String 3: G

Next, we'll learn the notes G and A on string 3.

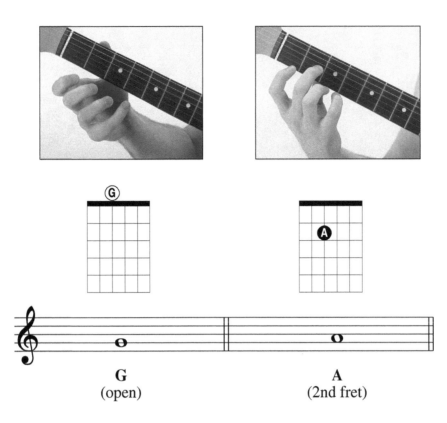

G
(open)

A
(2nd fret)

Practice G and A in the line below.

G–A Jam

The following tune uses notes on the first, second, and third strings.

Aura Lee

Eighth Notes

Eighth notes have a flag attached to their stems: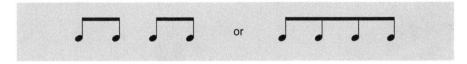

Two eighth notes equal the time value of a single quarter note. When several eighth notes appear together, their flags are joined together into a beam to make them easier to read.

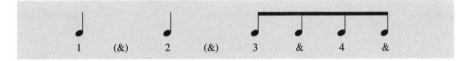

To count eighth notes, we divide the beat in half and use "and" between each beat:

Eighth rests also last a half-beat each.

The example below uses eighth notes and rests. The count is written below the notes.

The song below uses a **pickup measure**. This is a partial measure at the beginning of a song, which simply omits any opening rests. The two-note "pickup" below comes in on beat 4.

Snake Charmer

String 4: D

The following photos and diagrams show how to play the notes D, E, and F on the fourth string.

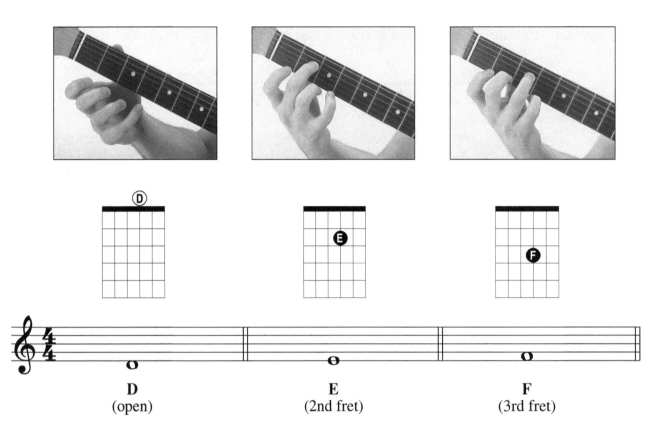

D
(open)

E
(2nd fret)

F
(3rd fret)

The following example uses only the three notes D, E, and F.

D–E–F Jam

The melody below uses notes on the fourth string. It is in 3/4 time. Notice that each measure contains only three beats.

House of the Rising Sun

More Sharps and Flats

The following photos and diagrams show how to play F♯, G♯, and B♭.

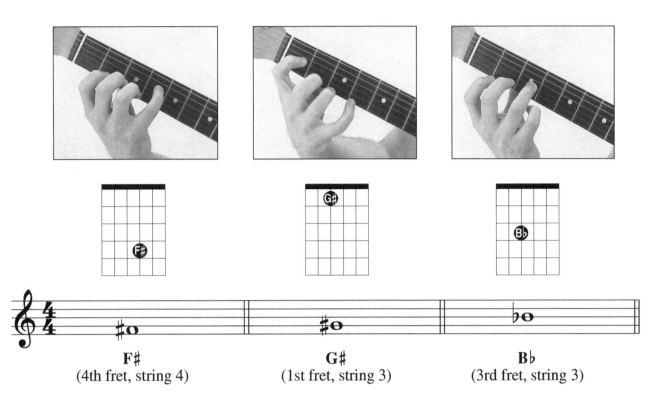

F♯
(4th fret, string 4)

G♯
(1st fret, string 3)

B♭
(3rd fret, string 3)

The following examples incorporate these new notes. The symbol :‖ means to repeat from the beginning of the piece. Remember, the natural sign (♮) cancels a previous sharp or flat.

Hard Rock Riff

Eastern Rock Riff

Bach Riff

Mystical Riff

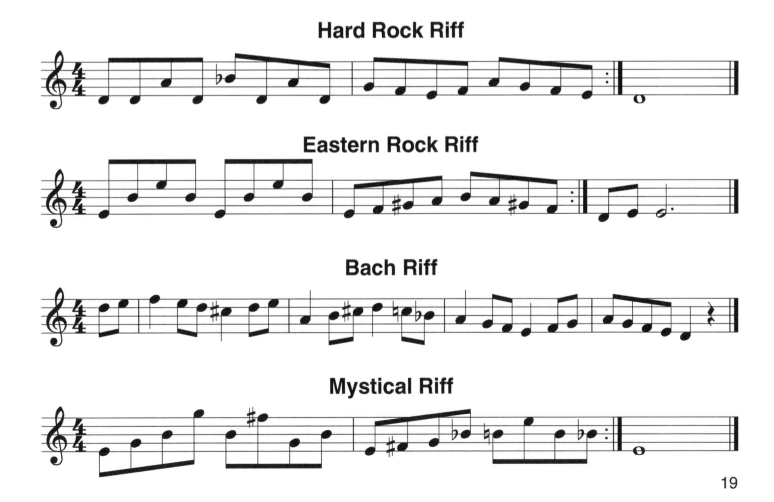

19

String 5: A

The following photos and diagrams show how to play A, B, and C, on the fifth string.

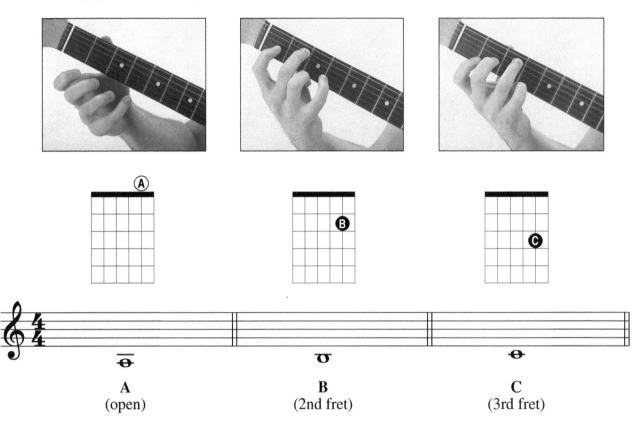

A	**B**	**C**
(open)	(2nd fret)	(3rd fret)

The following example uses the new notes A, B, and C.

A–B–C

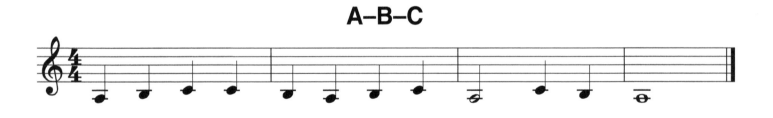

Now let's mix them in with higher notes.

Run, Don't Walk

C♯ is also found on the fifth string.

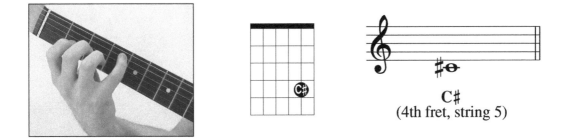

C♯
(4th fret, string 5)

The song "Greensleeves" uses the low C♯ note shown above as well as several **ties**. A tie (⌣) simply connects two or more notes together and tells you to let the first note ring through until the end of the last note. In other words, two tied notes are played as if they were one long note. (Whenever a sharp or flat note is tied, the sharp or flat is *not* restated.)

Greensleeves

String 6: E

The following photos and diagrams show how to play E, F, and G, on the sixth string.

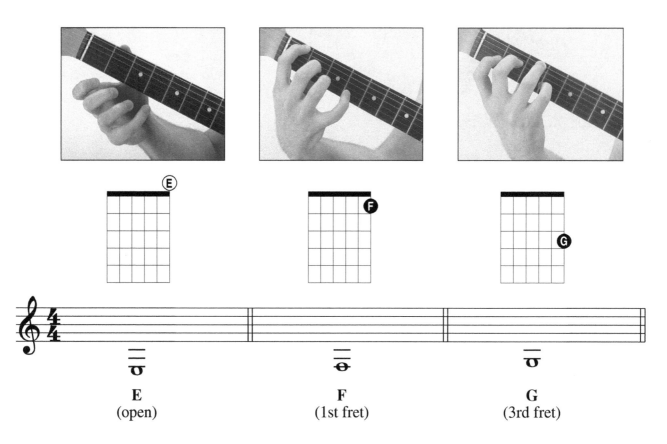

E
(open)

F
(1st fret)

G
(3rd fret)

The following example uses the low E, F, and G notes only.

Sixth-String Strut

Now let's mix them in with higher notes.

Battle Hymn

More Flats

Here are two more flats to learn, both at the first fret.

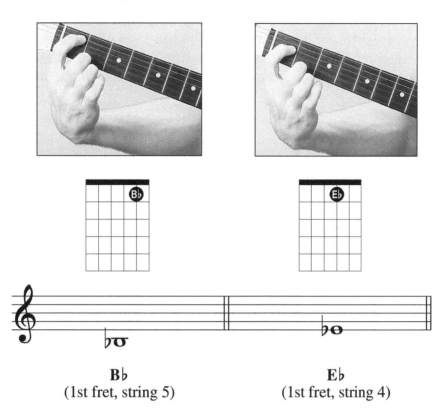

B♭
(1st fret, string 5)

E♭
(1st fret, string 4)

The tune below incorporates both B♭ and E♭.

Minor Jam

Strumming-Style Notation

In the previous section, the examples you played were all single-note melodies. Typically, however, the guitar part in a song will utilize **chords** to accompany a vocalist, who will sing the melody. Chords are particular combinations of notes played simultaneously. Here we will learn about open chords, progressions, strumming patterns, and common methods of their notation. Musical styles that commonly rely on strumming patterns and open chords include folk, pop, and rock.

Reading chord boxes

When fingerboard grids are used to show chord shapes, they are commonly called chord "boxes." Just as before, the vertical lines represent the strings, and the horizontal lines indicate the frets. The dots on the grid show where to put your fingers. In addition, a small "o" above a string means to play it open. An "x" above a string means to avoid strumming it (or hold it mute so that it can't ring). And the numbers across the bottom indicate which finger to use on each string (1 = index, 2 = middle, 3 = ring, 4 = pinkie).

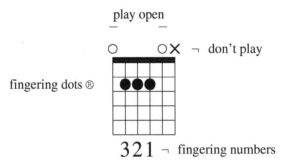

Open Major Chords

There are five common open chord shapes—E, A, D, G, and C. The designation "open" simply means that the shapes incorporate open strings. They are all **major** chord types, which we'll elaborate on in a moment. Practice strumming each chord until you have the shapes memorized. Also, pick the strings individually so that you can hear if they are each sounding correctly. Try to eliminate any string "buzz" or unintentionally deadened strings.

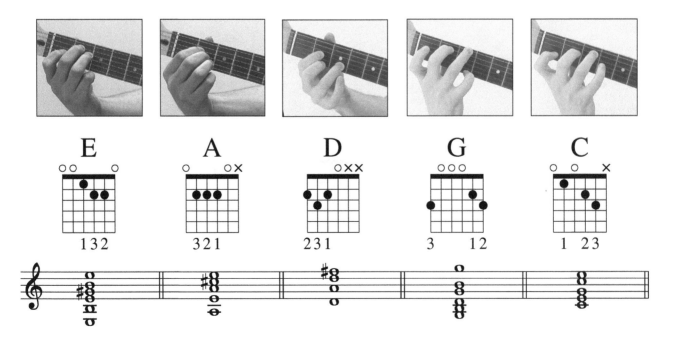

Slash Notation

Although chords can be written on the staff, it quickly becomes apparent that reading all the notes contained in each chord is relatively difficult. It is far easier to simply indicate the chord shape, and then show the rhythmic values of each chord strum.

To do this, a method of musical shorthand has been devised called **slash notation**. It uses a type of "slashed" notehead to indicate a full chord strum on a given chord. In its simplest form, the rhythm appears as a series of "hash marks," which simply indicate one strum per beat (quarter notes). Practice the progression below, which uses this type of notational shorthand.

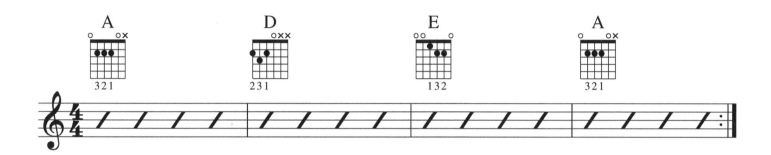

You don't always need to play quarter notes, though, when you see hash marks. Often they are meant to "stand in" for any rhythm, and simply indicate the number of beats you should remain on each chord. In other words, the specific strumming rhythm is left up to you. There *is* a way, however, that specific rhythms can be conveyed with slash notation. The hash marks can sprout stems. Below, a rhythm is applied to each chord of the progression using this type of rhythmic slash notation.

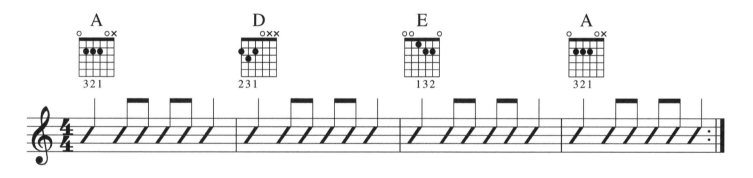

When the staff contains a vocal line or other guitar part, the slash notation may appear above it, entirely outside the staff.

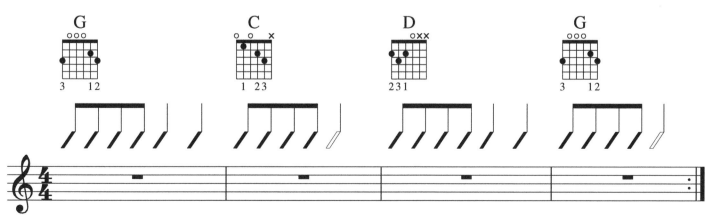

Time Values

You should already be familiar with the basic time values of notes from the previous section. Here we will briefly summarize them and add a few more.

Remember, rhythmic values can be added together like fractions (e.g., a quarter plus a quarter equals a half; an eighth plus an eighth equals a quarter). The "note pyramid" below shows the relative equivalent time values for each type of note, beginning with the whole note and continuing down to **sixteenth notes** (with double beams). By the way, an easy way to remember that a *whole* note lasts four beats is to think of it as filling up a *whole* measure, which it does in 4/4 time.

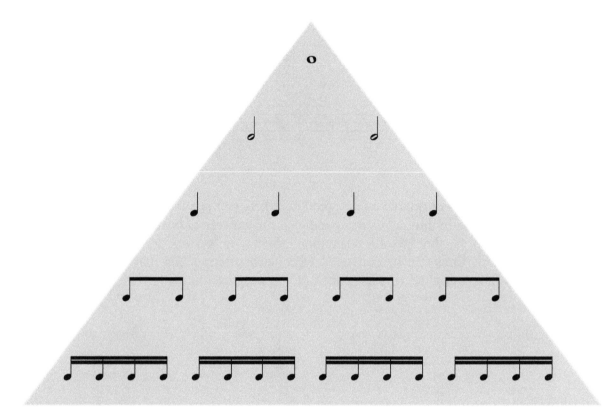

As you already know, a dot placed after a half note makes it equal to three full beats, instead of just two. In addition, dots may be placed after other types of notes as well. The rule is: a dot adds half the value of the original note to itself. So a **dotted quarter note** lasts one and a half beats, or the length of a quarter note plus an eighth note. A **dotted eighth note** lasts three quarters of a beat, or the length of an eighth note plus a sixteenth note.

Syncopation

For our purposes, a **syncopated rhythm** is one in which an upbeat (that's the "and" halfway between beats) is played, then held over the following downbeat. A tie (⌣) symbol connects notes together, so they are played as if they were one long note.

After you play the "and" of beat 2, miss the strings on the next downstroke (beat 3), then catch the following upstroke. The picking is shown above the staff.

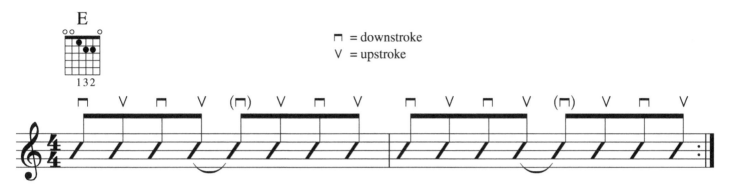

To develop a good feel for rhythm and timing, it is good practice to mark time by tapping your foot evenly and consistently with the beat. Practice the following chord changes, tapping your foot steadily on each numbered downbeat. The count, or beat, is shown below the staff. Go slowly at first.

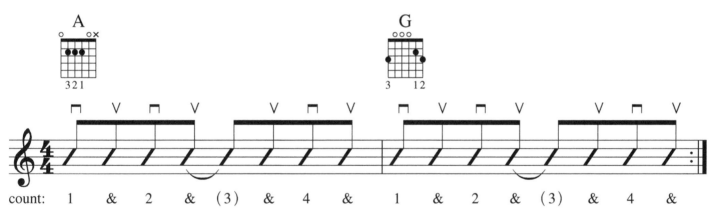

The syncopation may appear at any point in the measure. The chord boxes are omitted below, as by now you should have these shapes memorized. Refer back to page 24 if you need a reminder.

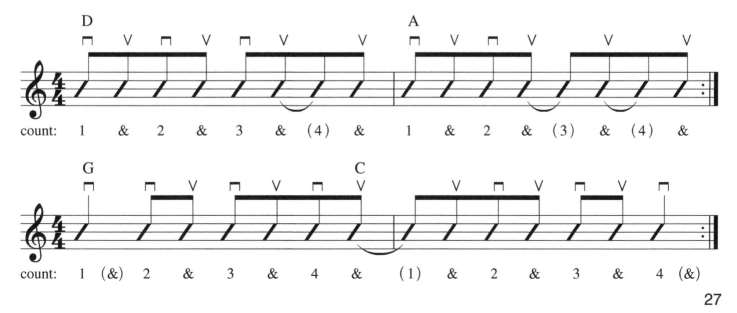

Open Minor Chords

Each chord also has a minor version, designated by adding a small "m" after its letter name. Minor chords have a different "color" than their major counterparts. E minor, A minor, and D minor are shown below. After you learn them, play the major version of each chord followed by its minor version and notice the similarity. In each case, only one note is altered to transform each chord from major to minor. Also listen for the change of chord color as you play first major, then minor. (G minor and C minor do not have convenient open shapes, so we will skip them for now.)

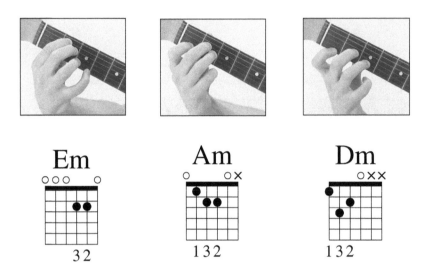

The following progressions use minor chords as well as some major chords. To help make the transitions between chords easier, it is common to hit several open strings on the last eighth note of each measure, while your right hand finds the next chord shape. It doesn't really matter exactly which strings you hit. Try these progressions using "open-string transitions," maintaining a steady eighth-note rhythm in your strumming.

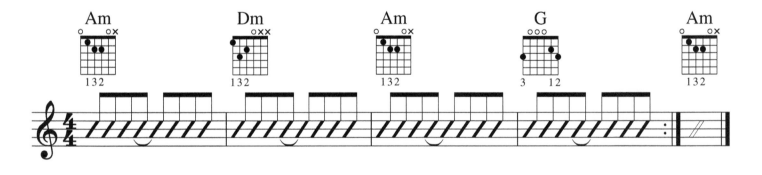

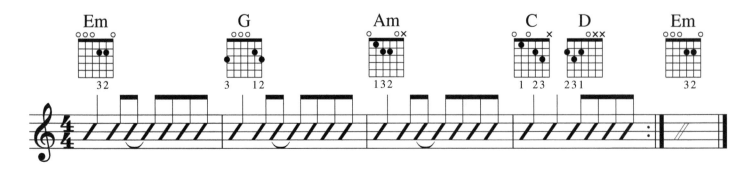

Open Seventh Chords

Dominant seventh chords provide yet another type of chord "color." The dominant seventh is also known as simply a "7th" chord, and is indicated with the suffix "7" following the letter name of the chord. Below are the open position seventh chords. Notice their similarity to the major chords of the same letter name. In each case, only one note is altered.

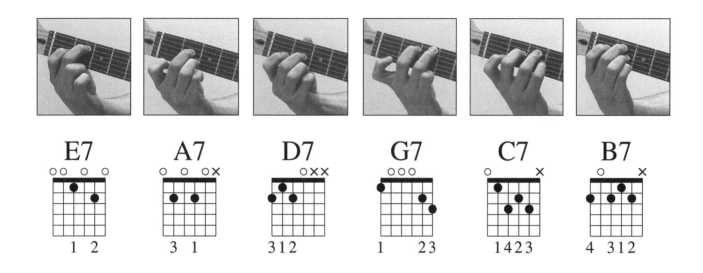

The following progressions incorporate dominant seventh chords.

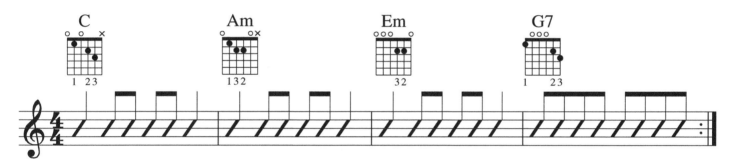

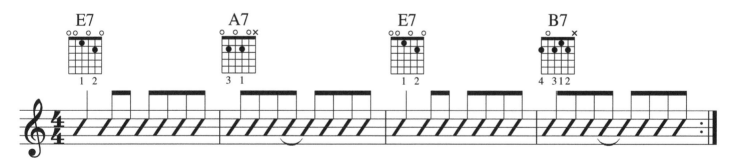

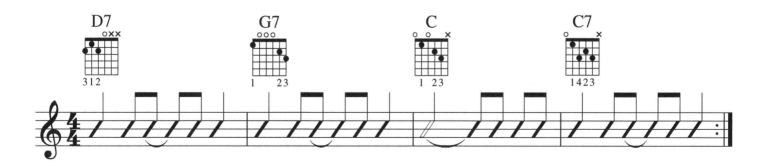

Strumming Patterns

Certain rhythms, or **strumming patterns**, are commonly seen in guitar accompaniment styles. We will start simple and build up from there. Some patterns may be review from the previous pages. You should concentrate on keeping an even, steady beat as you tap your foot, and practice each strum until it feels comfortable. At this point, you should ideally have the chords memorized; refer back to the appropriate page to review them if necessary. Remember, you can use open-string transitions between chord changes.

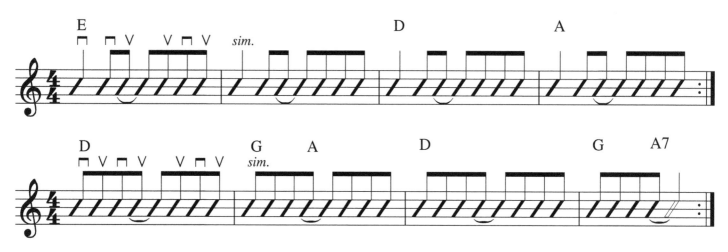

The next two examples use longer, eight-measure progressions.

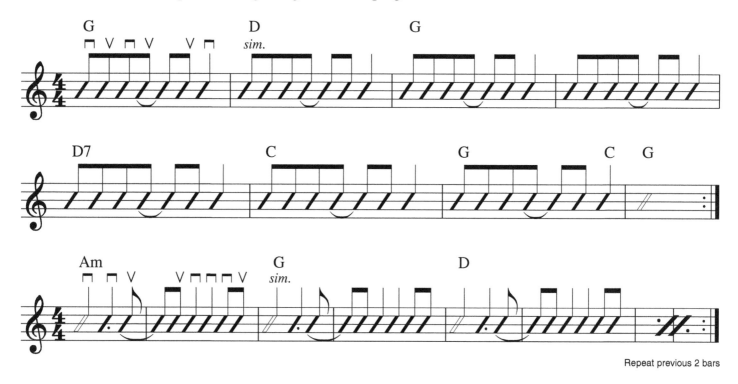

Repeat previous 2 bars

Here is a strumming pattern in 3/4 time.

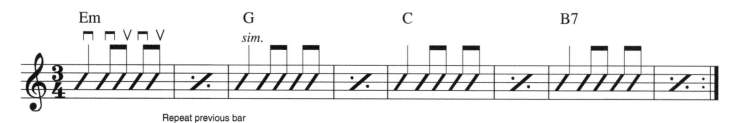

Repeat previous bar

Sixteenth notes are twice the speed of eighth notes. The following example utilizes a sixteenth-note strumming rhythm. This subdivides the beat into four parts, which is commonly vocalized "**one**-ee-and-uh, **two**-ee-and-uh, **three**-ee-and-uh, **four**-ee-and-uh." Also, we will use all downstrokes to play eighth notes now, since the faster sixteenth notes will use alternate down/up/down/up picking.

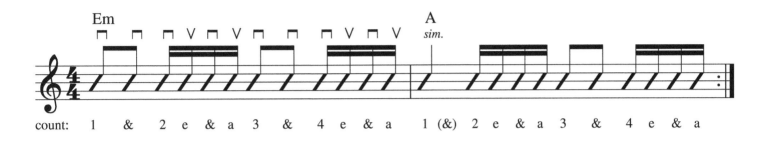

Sixteenth notes may also be syncopated. This is harder than the previous strumming patterns, but there is a way to make it seem easier. In the staves below, notice that both rhythms are identical except that the top one is in eighth notes and the bottom one is in sixteenths. If you played the second line at exactly half the tempo (speed) of the first line, the rhythms would sound identical.

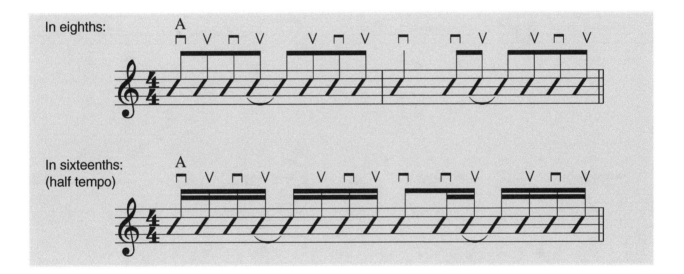

One good way to tackle any complex sixteenth-note rhythm is to double the speed of the beat (double time), thereby transforming it into an eighth-note rhythm. Then after you've learned the rhythm, just tap your foot half as fast (on every other beat) and your eighth-note rhythm will be transformed back into sixteenth notes! Use this approach on the following rhythm if you have trouble. The normal count (sixteenth notes) is shown below, followed by the double-time count (eighth notes).

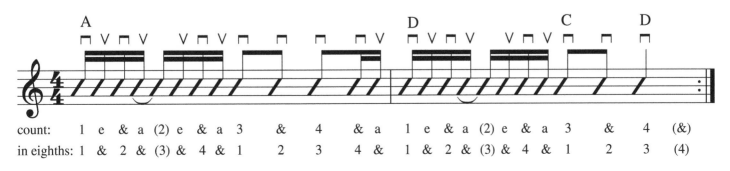

Root/Chord Strumming

Another strumming approach is to first pick only the low root note of each chord (the note with the same letter name as the chord), followed by full chord strums. This is common in country and western as well as folk guitar styles. The single notes are written on the staff normally, followed by slash notation indicating chord strums.

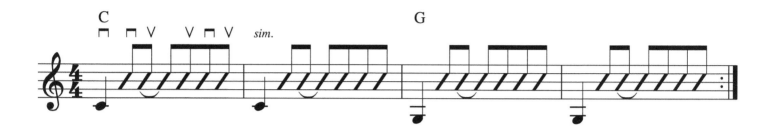

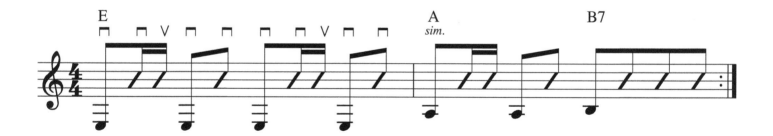

Remember, a dotted eighth note is the length of an eighth note plus a sixteenth—in other words, three-quarters of a beat. Notice the count below the next example.

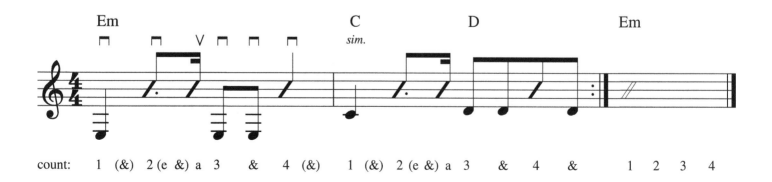

count: 1 (&) 2 (e &) a 3   &   4 (&)   1 (&) 2 (e &) a 3   &   4   &   1   2   3   4

Vocal Accompaniment

As mentioned earlier, vocal accompaniment is one of the main functions of the guitar. For the song below, practice strumming the chords while you *sing* the vocal line written in the staff. If you aren't familiar with the song's melody already, simply play the melody on the guitar a number of times, and sing along until you learn it. Then practice the strumming rhythm with the chords shown. Finally, put the pieces together, strumming the chords as you sing the melody. It takes a little practice to learn to do both things simultaneously, but with a little effort, you'll get it. Start with the strumming pattern shown, but don't hesitate to alter it as you see fit.

Scarborough Fair

Reading Tablature

Another common type of notation used for guitar is **tablature**, or **TAB** for short. Like standard staff notation, this system has also been around for centuries. It is particularly effective for fretted, stringed instruments such as the guitar. The fact that more guitarists read tablature than any other type of notation is a testament to its usefulness.

The TAB staff

In the tablature system, a six-line staff represents the strings on the guitar, one line for each string. Numbers appear on the lines and indicate the frets to be played. The spaces are not used.

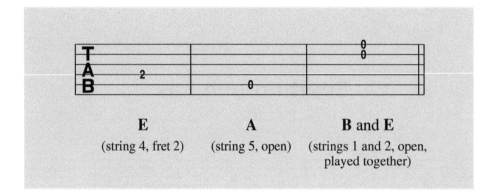

Tablature may appear by itself, but it is more commonly used in conjunction with a staff. Although the TAB shows exactly where the correct pitches are to be found on the guitar, you must still look at the staff to find the rhythmic values of the notes. Also, the staff can give you special information that might not be clear in the TAB, such as the key or important note relationships.

A Single Staff-TAB System

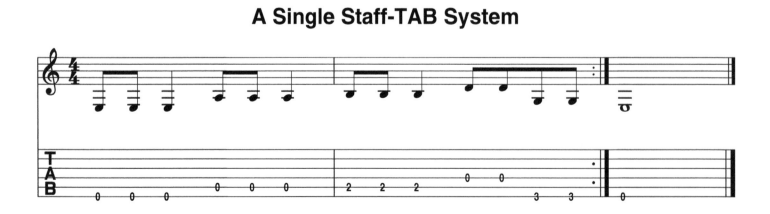

34

Boogie Patterns in E

The following rhythm figures are said to be "in the key of E." This means that the pitch E is the tonal center; it's the "home base" note that the other notes gravitate toward and ultimately want to come to rest on. These single-note patterns are called **boogie patterns** because they are common to a form of early rock 'n' roll known as "boogie woogie." In this style, these figures are generally played in the piano bass line and doubled with guitar. They are shown in full staff-TAB systems.

Each is played in **second position**. This means that your first finger plays all notes on the *second* fret, your second finger plays notes on the *third* fret, your third finger plays notes on the *fourth* fret, and your fourth finger plays notes on the *fifth* fret. Also, when a note is sharped, all subsequent appearances of the same letter-name pitch in that measure are likewise sharped. If a following note of the same letter name is meant to be played "unsharped," a natural sign is used.

Boogie Pattern #1

Boogie Pattern #2

Boogie Pattern #3

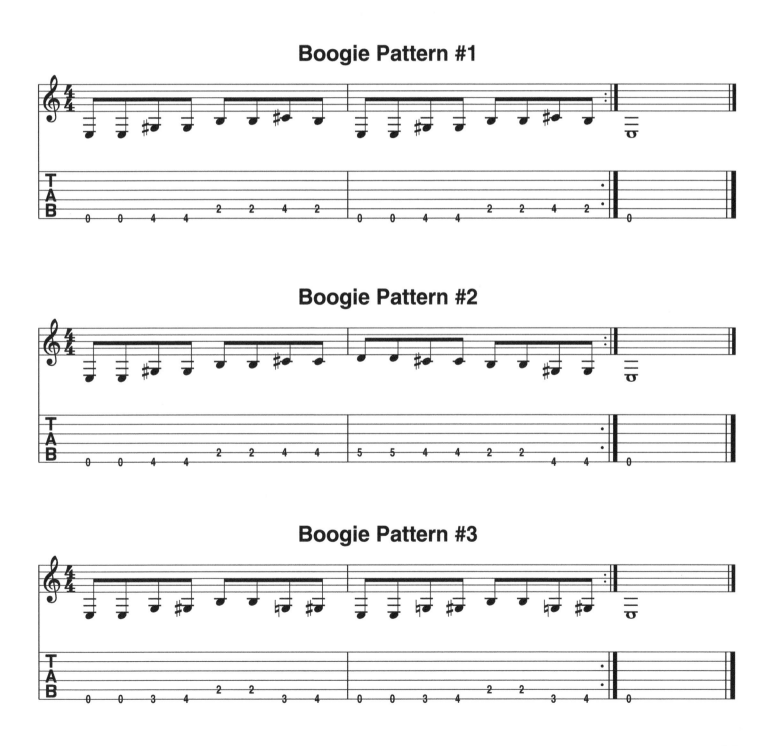

Single-Note Riffs

The previous boogie patterns could also be called "riffs," since a **riff** is any short repeating phrase that plays a significant role in a song. The term riff, however, is typically used in reference to later rock styles. Below are several single-note rock riffs, in several different keys.

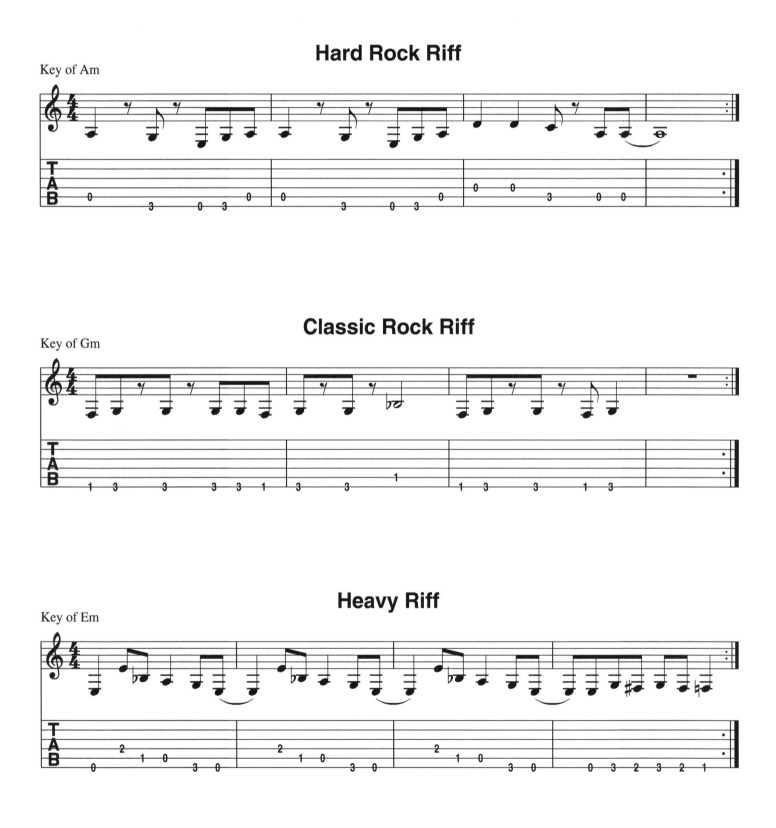

Hard Rock Riff
Key of Am

Classic Rock Riff
Key of Gm

Heavy Riff
Key of Em

Arpeggiated Chords

When the notes of a chord are played one note after another, in sequence, they are called an **arpeggio**. Practice picking the individual notes of each chord in the following examples. In this style of accompaniment, we hold each chord shape throughout its arpeggiated sequence and let the strings ring together.

Technically, this approach lies somewhere in between arpeggios and chords. Although the notes are picked individually (as an arpeggio), they are allowed to ring together (as a chord). Therefore, this approach is best described as playing "arpeggiated chords." It is also known as playing "broken chords," particularly when the pattern includes two or more strings played together, as in the last example above.

Power Chords and Riffs

Power chords omit the note that normally colors a chord major or minor—the 3rd. This gives them a "hollow-sounding," or "powerful," quality. Power chords are common in hard rock and metal guitar styles and are especially effective when played with a distorted guitar tone. However, they are equally viable when played on acoustic guitar. A number "5" following the chord's letter name indicates that it is a power chord type.

Open Power Chords

Below, the open power chords E5, A5, and D5 are shown in their simplest two-string versions. Since you already know the full chord shapes, notice how the notes of the power chords are derived from them. Be careful to pick only the strings indicated. It is also helpful to lean the side of your first finger over enough to lightly touch and mute all the higher-sounding strings. On A5 and D5, you can also use your thumb over the top of the neck to hold the low string(s) quiet.

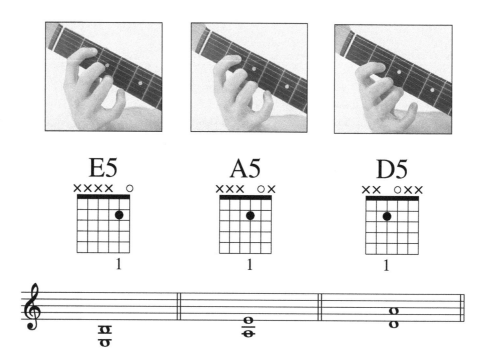

This hard rock-style chordal riff uses open power chords. Use your thumb over the top of the neck to touch and mute the sixth string on A5, and the sixth and fifth strings on D5. Use all downstrokes.

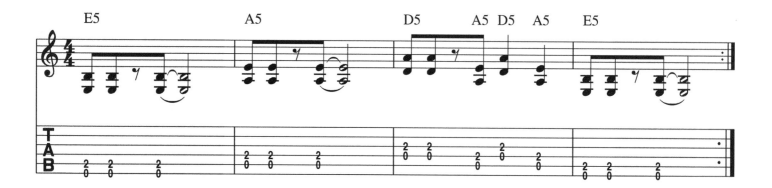

Extended Open Power Chords

The previous power chords may be extended into the three-string versions shown below. The "barre symbol," which looks like a tie, indicates that your finger should lay flat and fret both strings at the indicated position. Also, open G5 is shown, which uses more strings and requires that you mute string 5 with the side of your middle finger.

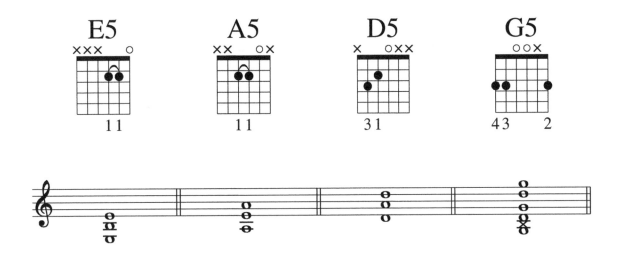

The following examples use these fuller power chord shapes. Play the G notes in measure 4 with your second (middle) finger.

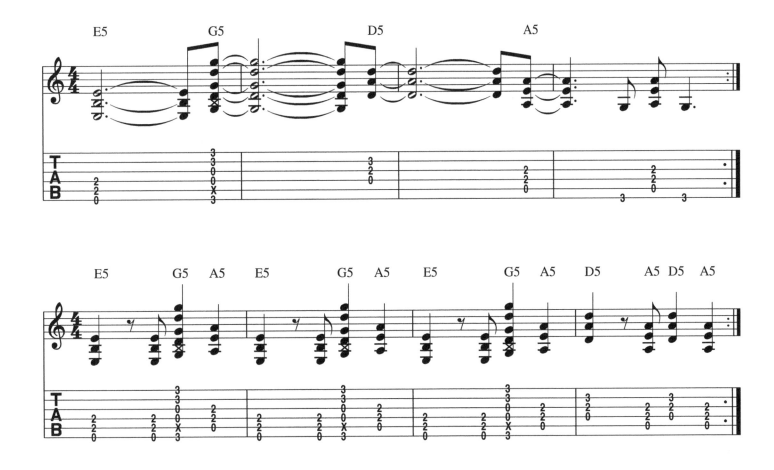

Movable Power Chords

The power chord shapes may be raised up the fretboard to play power chords with different letter names (i.e., F5, F♯5, G5, G♯5, A5, A♯5, B5, C5, etc.). Moving the E5 and A5 shapes up the neck yields these movable shapes, shown here at the first fret.

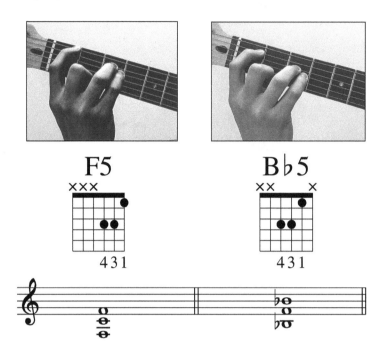

In each case, the root of the chord is played with your first finger, and it names the chord. Now if you learn the names of the notes on the sixth and fifth strings, shown in the neck diagram below, you can play any power chord simply by sliding the appropriate movable shape to the appropriate fret. (The notes in the intervening spaces are named with sharps or flats.) Play up and down the fretboard, saying the note names out loud until they are memorized.

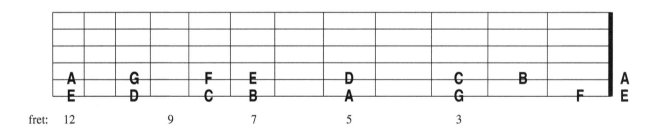

Practice the following riff using movable power chords.

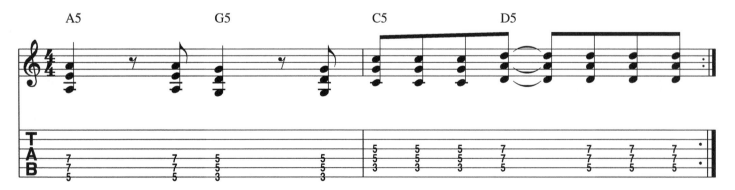

40

Guitar Articulations

Hammer-ons

The following riffs combine single-note and power-chord textures. They also incorporate some special articulation techniques, the first of which is the **hammer-on**. When two notes are connected with a slur symbol (⌣), it means that the second note is not picked. Instead, you should hammer your finger down on the string to sound that note without picking. (The slur symbol looks just like a tie, except that it connects notes that are *not* the same pitch.)

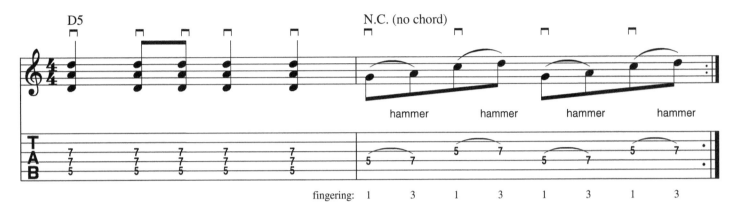

Pull-offs

A **pull-off** is essentially the opposite of a hammer-on. Again, two notes are shown connected with a slur symbol, but this time the second note is *lower* than the first. To sound the second note in the example below without picking, anchor both your first and third fingers on their respective frets, then pull your third finger slightly away from the fretboard and down to "pluck" the string and sound the second note without picking.

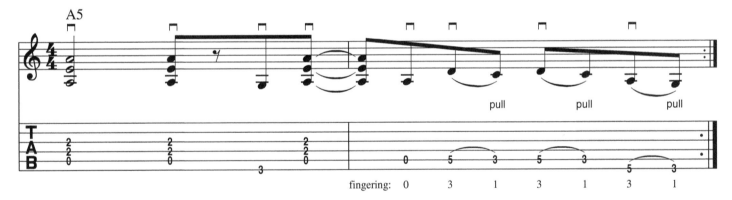

Palm muting

Palm muting is a technique that alters the tone of notes, giving them a muffled sound. Lay the heel of your left hand over the ends of the strings at the bridge, so that the fleshy part is in contact with about a half inch of the strings. Now when you pick notes, they will sound short and percussive, dying away quickly. Palm muting is indicated with a small "P.M." under the staff.

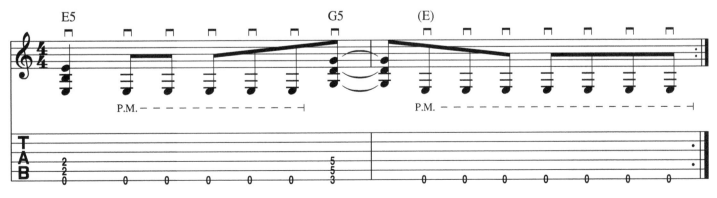

Barre Chords

When full major and minor chords are transformed into movable chord shapes, we call them **barre chords** (pronounced like "bar"). This is exactly the same principle as when we created movable power chords, except that this time we are using full chords. First, we will look at barre chords based on the shape of the open E chord.

E-form Barre Chords

Below are the movable E-form major and minor barre chord shapes based on the corresponding open chords. Notice that the fingerings change from that of the open chords to allow the first finger to barre across all six strings (effectively raising each open string in tandem with the other notes of the chord). Pick one string at a time to make sure that they are all sounding. Try to eliminate buzzing or deadened strings by adjusting your finger position and pressure on the fretboard.

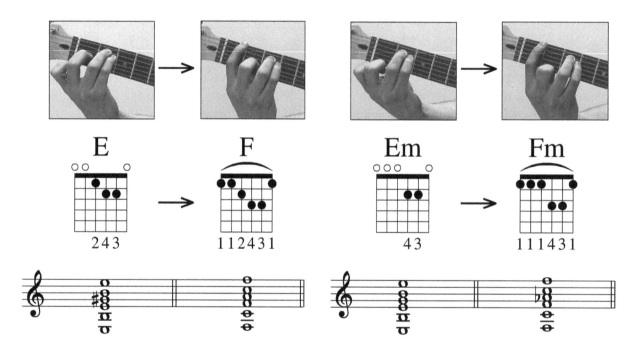

Just as before, these shapes can be moved up or down the fretboard to create a variety of major and minor chords. The fret that your first finger is on names the chord. (Refer back to page 40 if you need to review the note names on the sixth string.) The progression below uses these full E-form barre chords.

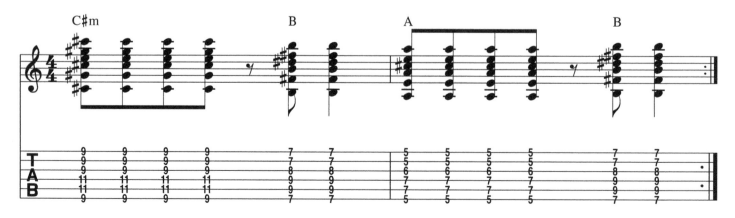

A-form Barre Chords

When we apply the same idea to the open A and Am chords, we create the A-form barre chords. Again, the fingerings have been changed from that of the standard open chords.

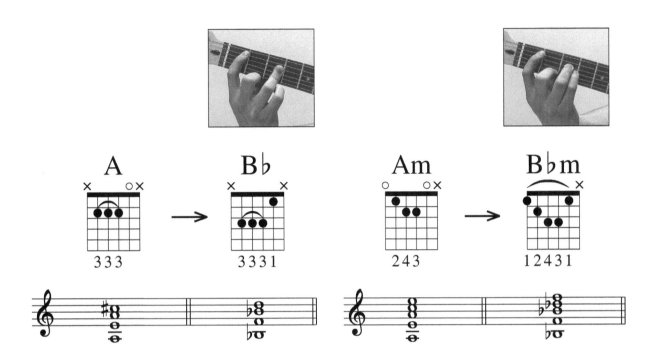

The progression below uses full A-form barre chords. Again, listen carefully for buzzing or unintentionally deadened strings.

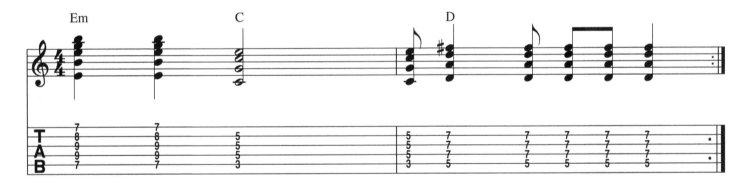

Now we'll mix E-form and A-form barre chords together.

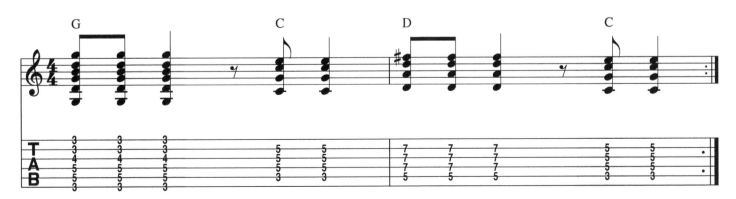

Progressions

The following progressions incorporate barre chords. They are written using chord boxes and slash notation. To depict regions higher on the neck, chord boxes include a fret number (e.g., "7 fr") next to the diagram.

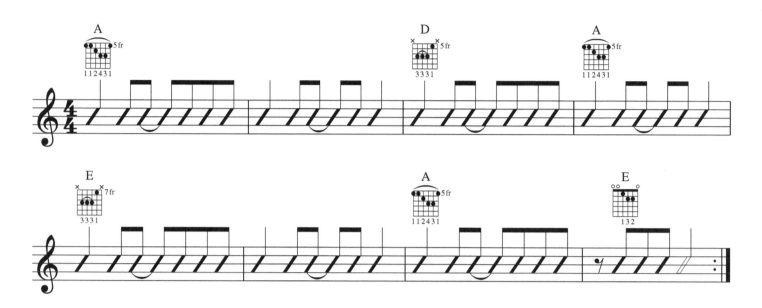

When an "X" appears in place of noteheads or slashes, it means that you should release pressure off the strings so that they produce only a percussive "click" when struck. Don't lift all the way off the strings, though, or they will ring open. In the following example, these "X" slashes function to ease the chord transitions. Change to the next chord during the Xs.

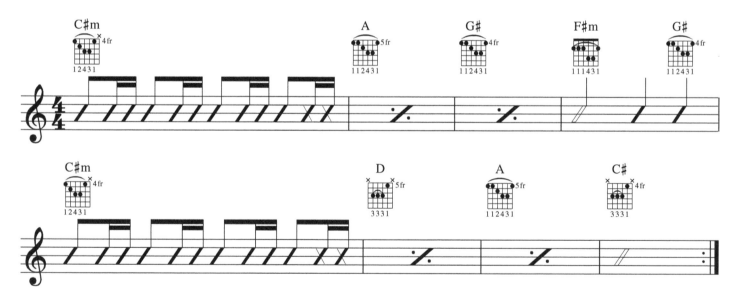

The progression below uses fret-hand muting for a rhythmic effect. It also requires more shifting.

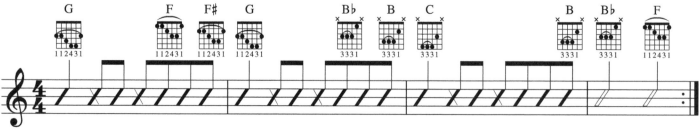

Seventh Barre Chords

Seventh chords may also be *barred* up the neck just like major and minor chords. Below are the movable E-form and A-form seventh chords (shown here at the first fret). These are a little harder to barre because the first finger must effectively hold down even more strings.

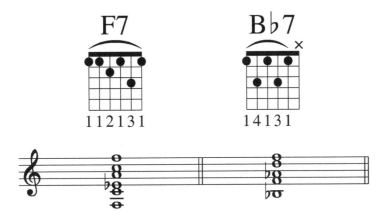

The following progression uses seventh barre chords.

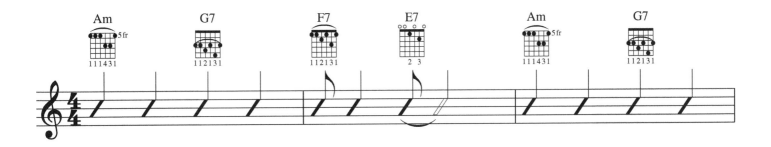

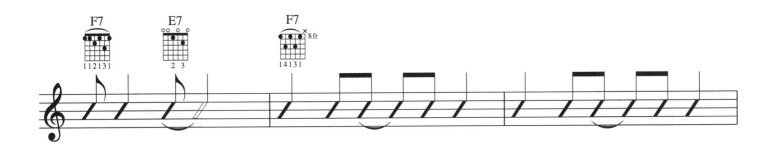

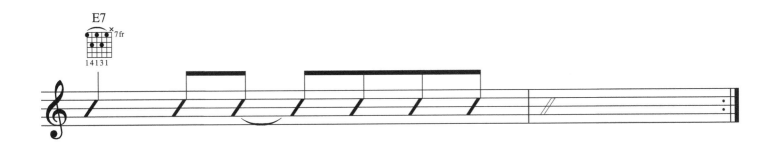

The Blues

The **blues** style lies at the foundation of many forms of rock and represents one of the most widely incorporated styles in modern music. Arising from the gospel and work songs of African-Americans in the post-Civil-War South, the blues gave voice to their hard life during those times. Later in the twentieth century, that voice broadened into a number of different offshoots. Today, we have Delta blues, electric blues, Chicago blues, Texas blues, blues-rock, blues-jazz, and more. One of the common threads of all these styles of blues is the heavy reliance on a 12-measure structure, the "12-bar blues progression."

The 12-Bar Blues Progression

Below is the basic 12-bar progression shown in the key of A. When A is the tonal center, the three chords in the progression are A, D, and E. The progression is made up of three phrases, each four measures in length:

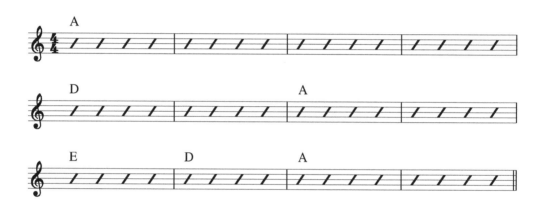

We commonly number the chords to reflect their *function*, or relationship to the tonal center, which in this case is A. Count up through the letter names to see what numbers are associated with A, D, and E.

A	B	C♯	D	E
1	2	3	4	5

Roman numerals are used to indicate chord relationships—so A is the I chord (pronounced "one chord"), D is the IV chord ("four chord"), and E is the V chord ("five chord"). The above 12-bar progression can then be represented with the following chord numerals:

I	I	I	I
IV	IV	I	I
V	IV	I	I

These numerals can indicate the same relative changes *in any key*. When the key is E, for example, E becomes the I chord, A is the IV chord, and B is the V chord.

E	F♯	G♯	A	B		E	E	E	E
1	2	3	4	5		A	A	E	E
						B	A	E	E

The Shuffle Rhythm

Another common characteristic of blues is the **shuffle rhythm**. This is a triplet-based rhythm, so let's first look at triplets. Triplets are three evenly spaced notes that occur in the space of one beat. They are generally counted, "one-trip-let, two-trip-let," etc.

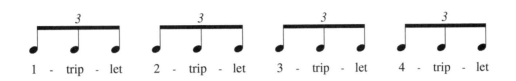

Now tie the first two notes of each group, picking only the first and third notes of each triplet. This creates the shuffle, or "swing" rhythm.

Since two tied eighths equal a quarter note, the shuffle rhythm can also look like this:

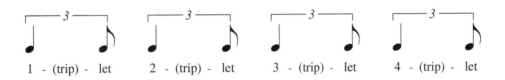

Sixth Comping

The term "comping" is an abbreviation for "accompanying." A *comping figure* is simply the name we give to an accompaniment rhythm figure in a particular style. In blues, the most common type of accompaniment is **sixth comping**, shown below. Use your first and third fingers to play the A5 dyad (a dyad is a two-note chord), then without lifting either finger, add your fourth finger to play the A6 dyad, as shown in the photo.

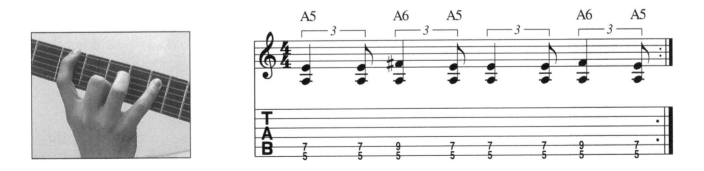

Sixth comping is also common in rock 'n' roll, although in that case the rhythm is usually played in up-tempo, straight eighth notes rather than a slower, blues shuffle.

Blues Shuffle

The blues shuffle below uses the 12-bar progression in A, with sixth comping throughout. Notice the overall chord relationships of I, IV, and V, written below the TAB line. A *turnaround* on V is added at the end, which "turns" the progression "around" to repeat from the beginning.

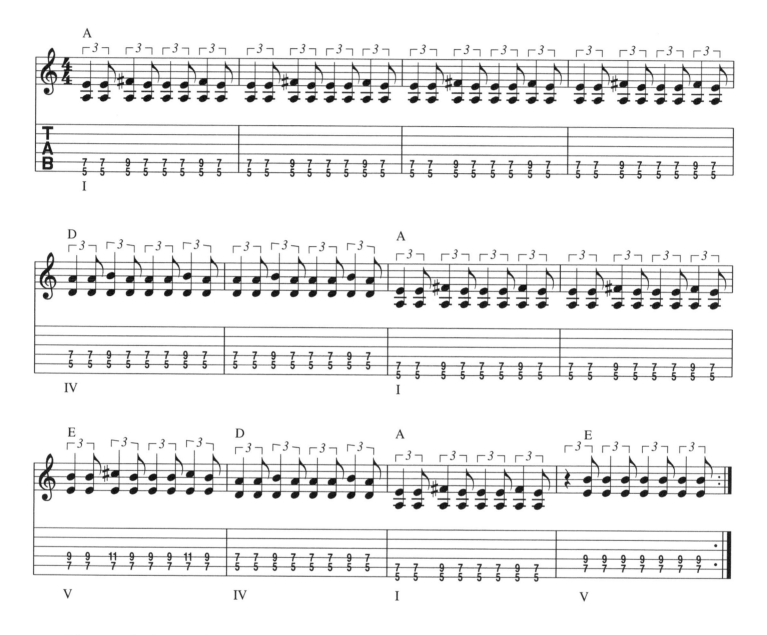

Now try playing the above blues shuffle in the key of G. Use the same comping figure, but apply it to the chords G (the new I chord), C (the new IV chord), and D (the new V chord). You'll notice that everything is simply shifted down two frets.

Finally, try the progression in the key of E (E=I, A=IV, and B=V). Here, the comping figure looks a little different since open strings are involved. On the right is the comping figure for the low E chord. Use your first and third fingers.

The Blues Scale

The blues scale is a type of minor scale. (See the scale reference starting on page 67 for more on this and other scales.) It is shown below based on the root note E. Memorize the shape and pattern of this scale.

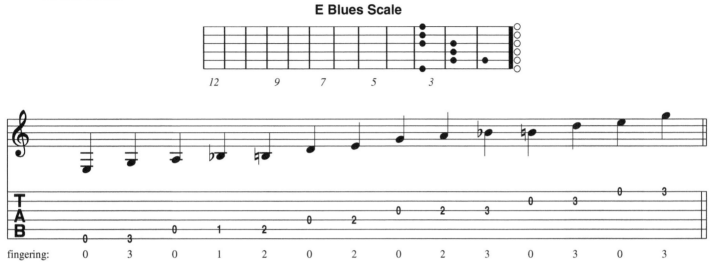

Here is the same scale in G. This version is a movable shape, just like the barre chords and movable power chords we saw earlier. The fingering is a little different since we are no longer using open strings.

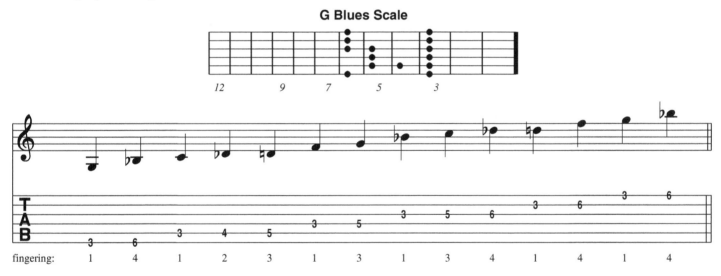

You can play this scale in any key just by sliding the entire shape up or down the neck, placing the first note of the scale shape on the new root. This scale is also useful for creating licks.

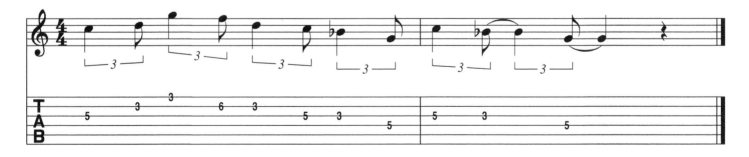

Texas Blues Shuffle

A common idea in the blues is the "call and response" pattern. Most often, this interplay will occur between the vocals and a lead guitar, which plays short fills that "answer" each vocal phrase. In the following Texas blues-type groove, a call-and-response form is used in which the lead phrases alternate with rhythm chords. Notice that these lead licks draw from the E blues scale that we just learned.

Instead of writing out the shuffle indication throughout the tune, the symbol ♫ = ♪♪ appears at the beginning. This tells you to swing the eighth notes and play them as a shuffle even though they are written as standard eighth notes. When you reach the repeat sign, go back to the forward repeat symbol ‖: rather than the pickup. Also, this tune uses different chord voicings for E7 and A7.

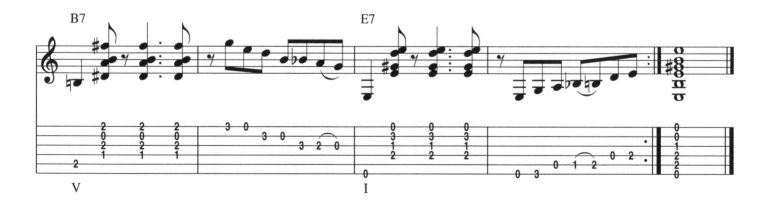

Fingerpicking Styles

So far, the pick has been used to sound the strings. In this section, we will focus on playing approaches that use the fingers of the left hand to pluck the strings. First, we will look at the basic fingerstyle approach, then we will consider hybrid picking.

The fingerstyle approach

The fingerstyle approach typically relies on the thumb to pluck the lower-sounding (bass) strings and the first three fingers to pluck the higher strings, although any fingers are free to pluck any string in certain circumstances. Classical (nylon-string) guitar generally relies on the fingers themselves to pluck the strings. Folk fingerstyle (steel-string) may use either the fingers or metal fingerpicks, attached to the thumb and fingers. In either case, both styles follow the same basic principle. Look at the following diagram and copy the position of the fingers and thumb.

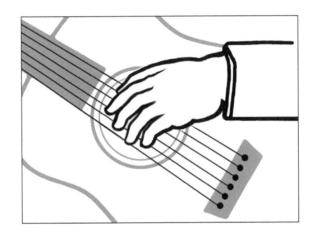

To designate the fingers and thumb of the picking hand, we use abbreviations of the Spanish words for them. (This helps keep us from confusing directions for the plucking hand with those for the fretting hand.) They are:

p	(for pulgar)	= thumb
i	(for indicio)	= index finger
m	(medio)	= middle finger
a	(anular)	= ring finger

Let's play an arpeggiated E major chord: the thumb (p) will pluck each note on strings 6, 5, and 4; the index finger (i) will take string 3; the middle finger (m) will take string 2; and the ring finger (a) will take string 1.

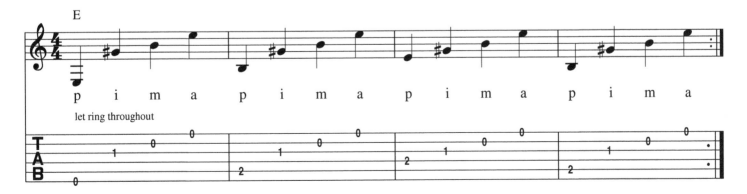

Common Arpeggiation Patterns

Practice the following arpeggiation patterns using the left-hand picking indications shown. Notice how the bass note (p) alternates between strings.

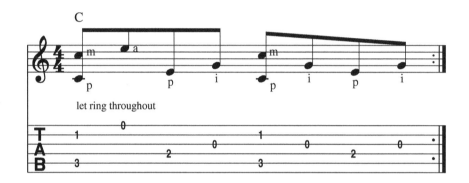

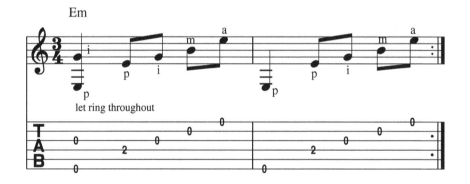

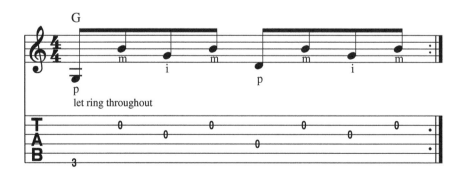

Fingerstyle Accompaniment

Now let's apply this fingerstyle approach to some chord progressions.

Below are the first five measures of "Scarborough Fair," which you played back on page 33, but shown here with a fingerstyle approach. Learn this pattern, then go back to page 33 and play the entire song fingerstyle. Feel free to alter this accompaniment pattern and create your own.

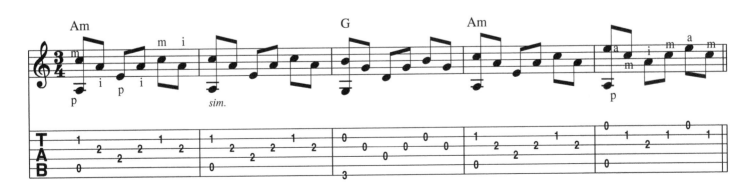

Ragtime

Ragtime is an American musical form that flourished in the early 1900s through the 1920s, at which time it began to be developed into a new style called jazz. Often played on piano or on acoustic fingerstyle guitar, ragtime typically consists of two voices (bass and midrange treble melodies) with prominent rhythmic syncopations. Here is the main theme of probably the most famous ragtime piece, "The Entertainer," by Scott Joplin. Play all the downstemmed notes with your thumb (p) and all the upstemmed notes with your fingers.

Hybrid Picking

Hybrid picking involves using a combination of the pick and the fingers. Hold the pick between your thumb and index finger, and use your middle and ring fingers to pluck additional strings. The first example below is a country-style progression using hybrid picking. The second is a rockabilly-style example also using hybrid picking. In each case, pick the bass notes with the pick, and pluck the highest two strings with your middle and ring fingers.

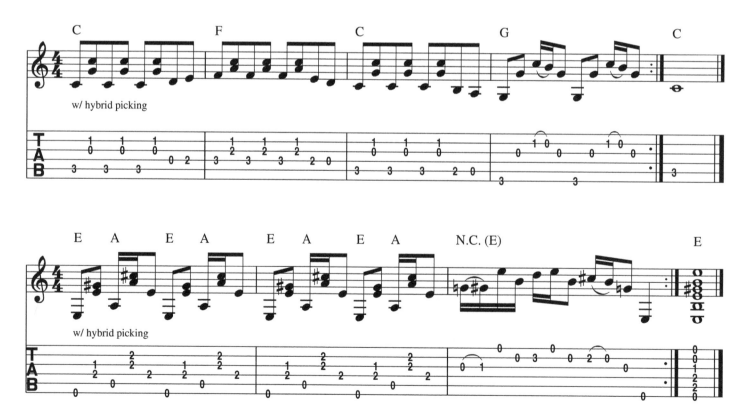

Classical

"Bourrée in E minor" by J. S. Bach demonstrates the classical fingerstyle approach. This piece is a little more difficult, as the two voices (melody and bass) move more independently. As is standard practice in classical guitar notation, the music is written in *divisi*, with the two voices appearing on one staff but with opposite stemming. Right-hand fingering numbers appear in the staff to help you with the unusual fingerings.

This piece also introduces the concept of a **key signature**. Every F note below is sharped, but rather than indicate this every time it occurs, the F line is sharped once at the beginning of every staff. This is a key signature. (Other sharps or flats that occur outside the key signature are called *accidentals*.) As its name suggests, the key signature can tell you what key the song is in. One sharp (F♯) indicates the key of either G major or E minor. In this case, it is E minor because the piece centers on the pitch E.

Bourrée in Em

(Strum with thumb)

Chord Reference

Open Chords

The twenty-one open position chord shapes for major, minor, and dominant seventh chords are shown below, using each of the natural note names (A–B–C–D–E–F–G). For a review on how to read chord boxes, see page 24.

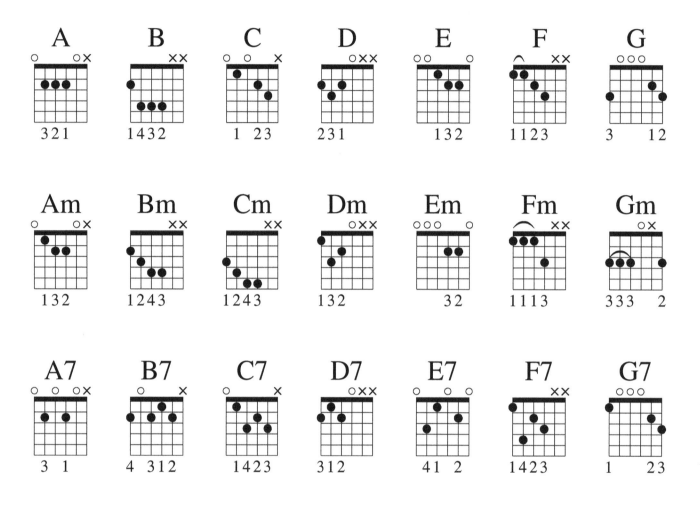

Here are the major seventh and minor seventh chord types in open position.

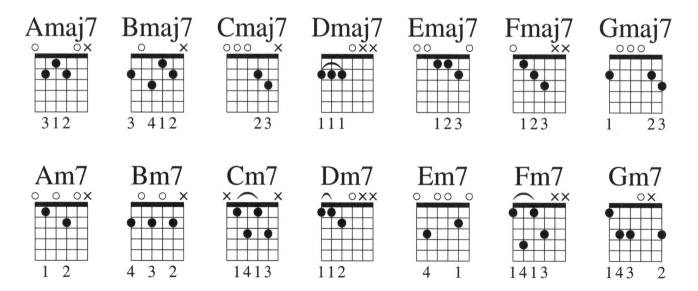

Movable Chord Shapes

The following pages contain movable chord shapes. These can be used to play chords of any letter name. The specific letter name of a chord is determined by the root note that the shape begins on. For example, the movable major chord shape shown below has its root on the sixth string.

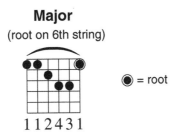

Major
(root on 6th string)

⊚ = root

1 1 2 4 3 1

If you play this shape beginning on the first fret, so that the note F occupies the position of the root, you have an F major chord. If you play this shape beginning on the second fret, so that the note F♯ occupies the position of the root, you have an F♯ major chord, and so on.

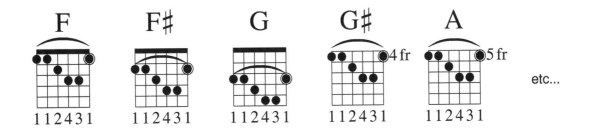

F	F♯	G	G♯	A
1 1 2 4 3 1	1 1 2 4 3 1	1 1 2 4 3 1	1 1 2 4 3 1	1 1 2 4 3 1

etc...

In order to use these movable shapes effectively, you will need to be able to find the note names on the guitar neck. Ideally, you should have them all memorized.

The notes on first twelve frets are shown in the diagram below. Above fret 12, the notes simply repeat, one octave higher. That is, fret 13 is the same as fret 1, but an octave higher; fret 14 is the same as fret 2, but an octave higher; and so on. Notes in between the natural letter names are named with sharps and flats. Each has two different names, the sharp of the letter name below it and the flat of the letter name above it. These two different names for the same pitch are called *enharmonic equivalents*.

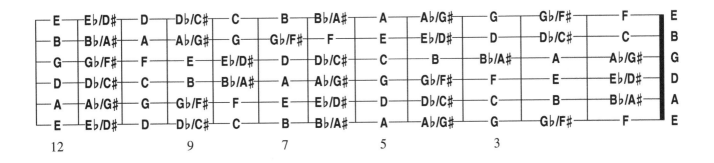

All natural notes (no flats or sharps in the name) are two frets (one whole step) apart—except for B–C and E–F, which are only one fret (one half step) apart.

Major (chord formula: 1 3 5)

Chords with no suffix are major types. The five movable major shapes can be referred to by the open shapes contained within them, giving us an "E-form," "D-form," "C-form," "A-form," and "G-form." Partial shapes derived from the full forms are on the second line. Don't confuse the shape, or "form," of the chord with its letter name. The shape only denotes what open chord the movable form *resembles*. The letter name is determined by the chord's position on the neck. (See page 57.) As an example, the neck diagram below shows all E major chords on the neck.

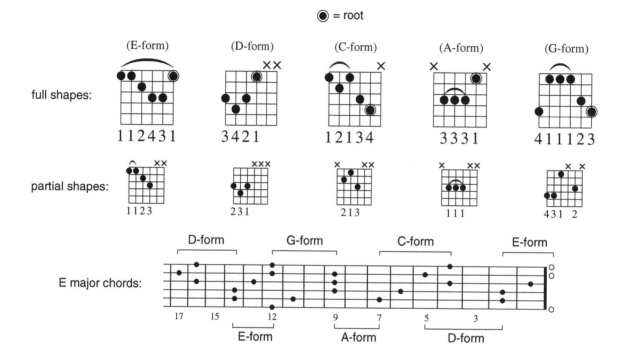

Minor (chord formula: 1 ♭3 5)

Minor chords are indicated with the suffix "m." The minor chord shapes work just like the majors, above. Again, the neck diagram shows how the full shapes appear on the neck, this time using Em chords as the example. To play other letter-named chords, position the root on the correct fret. (See page 57.)

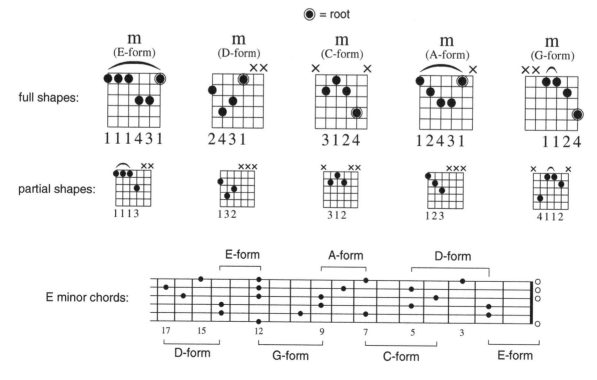

58

7th (chord formula: 1 3 5 ♭7)

Dominant 7th chords are commonly called simply "7th" chords, and labeled with the suffix "7." They consist of a major chord plus a minor 7th tone. Below are five different forms for 7th chords, corresponding to the five forms established on the previous page. To play specific letter-named chords with these forms, position the root on the correct note.

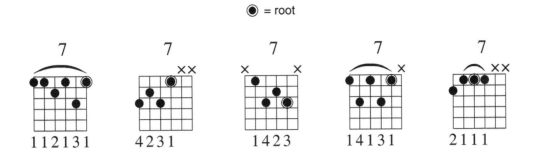

Major 7th (chord formula: 1 3 5 7)

Major 7th chords consist of a major chord with an added major 7th tone. They are labeled with the suffix "maj7." Below are five different forms of major 7th chords, corresponding to the five forms established on the previous page. To play specific letter-named chords with these forms, position the root on the correct note.

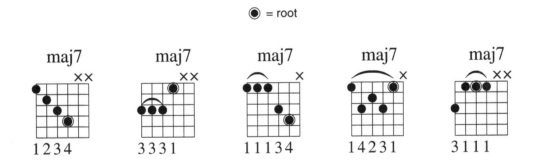

Minor 7th (chord formula: 1 ♭3 5 ♭7)

Minor 7th chords are labelled with the suffix "m7." They consist of a minor chord with an added minor 7th tone. Below are five different forms of minor 7th chords, corresponding to the five different forms established on the previous page. To play specific letter-named chords with these forms, position the root on the correct note.

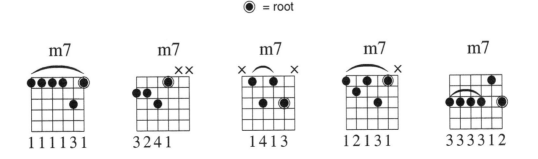

9th (chord formula: 1 3 5 ♭7 9)

A 9th chord is labeled with the suffix "9" and consists of a dominant 7th chord with an added 9th tone. Below are five different 9th forms, which correspond roughly to the five forms established previously on page 58. To play specific letter-named notes with these chord forms, position the root on the correct note.

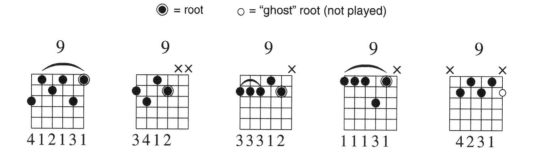

Major 9th (chord formula: 1 3 5 7 9)

Major 9th chords are labeled with the suffix "maj9" and consist of a major 7th chord with an added 9th tone. Below are five different major 9th forms, which correspond roughly to the five forms established on page 58. To play specific letter-named chords with these forms, position the root on the correct note.

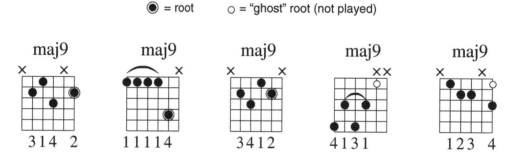

Minor 9th (chord formula: 1 ♭3 5 ♭7 9)

Minor 9th chords are labeled with the suffix "m9," and consist of a minor 7th chord with an added 9th tone. Below are five different forms of minor 9th chords. To play specific letter-named chords with these forms, position the root on the correct note.

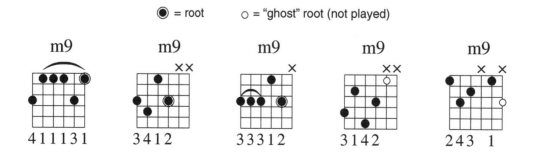

11th (chord formula: 1 3 5 ♭7 9 11)

An 11th chord is labeled with the suffix "11" and consists of a dominant 9th chord with an added 11th tone. Below are five different 11th forms, which correspond roughly to the five different forms established on page 58. (Note that some of the chord tones of these larger chords are routinely omitted.) To play specific letter-named chords with these forms, position the root on the correct note.

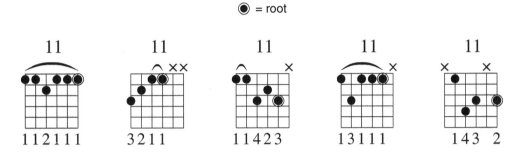

Minor 11th (chord formula: 1 ♭3 5 ♭7 9 11)

Minor 11th chords are labeled with the suffix "m11" and consist of a minor 9th chord with an added 11th tone. Below are five different minor 11th forms, which correspond roughly to the five forms established on page 58. To play specific letter-named chords with these forms, position the root on the correct note.

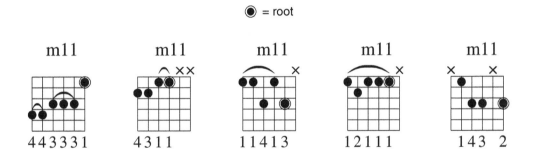

13th (chord formula: 1 3 5 ♭7 9 11 13)

A 13th chord is labeled with the suffix "13," and consist of an 11th chord with an added 13th tone. Below are five different forms of 13th chords which correspond roughly to the five forms established on page 58. (Note that some of the chord tones of these larger chords are routinely omitted.) To play specific letter-named chords with these forms, position the root on the correct note.

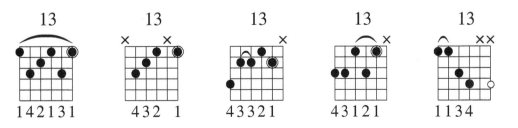

Power chords (chord formula: 1 5)

A power chord is labeled with the suffix "5" and consists of a root and 5th tone only. It can also be viewed as a major or minor chord without a 3rd tone. Below are five different power chord forms, which correspond to the five different forms established on page 58. To play specific letter-named chords with these forms, position the root on the correct note.

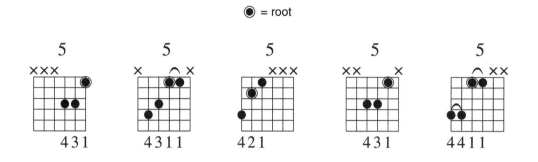

Suspended 4th (chord formula: 1 4 5)

A suspended 4th chord is labeled with the suffix "sus4" and consists of a major (or minor) chord in which the 3rd tone has been replaced with a 4th tone. Below are five different sus4 forms, which correspond roughly to the five different forms established on page 58. To play a specific letter-named chord with these forms, position the root on the correct note.

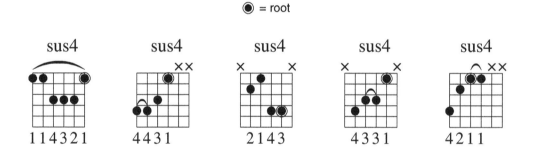

Suspended 2nd (chord formula: 1 2 5)

A suspended 2nd chord is labeled with the suffix "sus2" and consists of a major (or minor) chord in which the 3rd tone has been replaced with a 2nd tone. Below are five different sus2 forms, which correspond to the five different forms established on page 58. To play specific letter-named chords with these forms, position the root on the correct note.

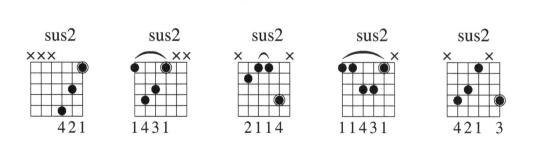

Added 9th (chord formula: 1 3 5 9)

An added 9th chord is labeled with the suffix "add9" and consists of a major chord with an added 9th tone. (Note that the straight 9th chord includes the 7th as well.) Add9 is similar to sus2, as the 9th and 2nd tones are identical. However, technically, add9 chords should also include a 3rd tone, whereas sus2 do not. Below are five different add9 forms, which correspond roughly to the five forms established on page 58. To play specific letter-named chords with these forms, position the root on the correct note.

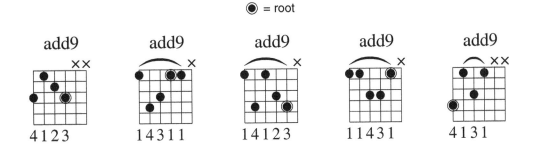

Minor added 9th (chord formula: 1 ♭3 5 9)

A minor added 9th chord is labeled with the suffix "m(add9)" and consists of a minor chord with an added 9th tone. Below are five different m(add9) forms, which correspond roughly to the five forms established on page 58. To play a specific letter-named chord with these forms, position the root on the correct note.

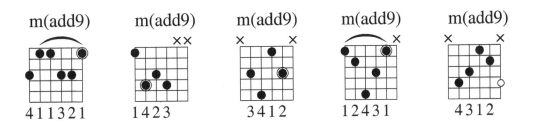

7th suspended 4th (chord formula: 1 4 5 ♭7)

A 7th suspended 4th chord is labeled with the suffix "7sus4" and consists of a dominant 7th chord in which the 3rd tone has been replaced with a 4th tone. Below are five different 7sus4 forms, which correspond to the five forms established on page 58. To play specific letter-named chords with these forms, position the root on the correct note.

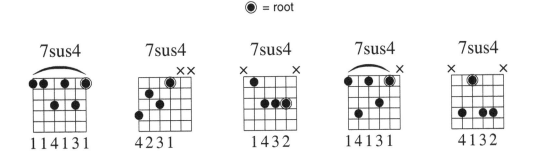

Diminished (chord formula: 1 ♭3 ♭5)

A diminished chord is labeled with the suffix "dim" or the symbol "°" and consists of a minor chord with a lowered 5th tone. Below are five different diminished forms, which corresond to the five different forms established on page 58. To play specific letter-named chords with these forms, position the root on the correct note.

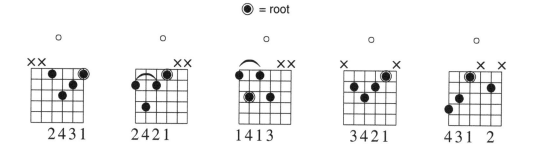

Diminished 7th (chord formula: 1 ♭3 ♭5 ♭♭7)

A diminished 7th chord is labeled with the suffix "dim7" or "°7" and consists of a diminished chord with an added doubled-flatted 7th tone. Below are five different diminished 7th forms, which correspond to the five different forms established on page 58. In addition, each of these forms may be shifted up or down the neck in three-fret intervals, creating a different voicing of the same diminished 7th chord. To play specific letter-named chords with these forms, position the root on the correct note.

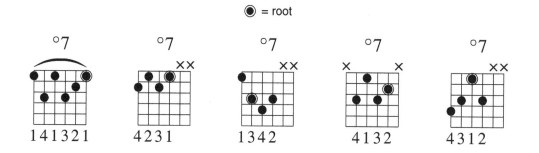

Minor 7th flat 5th (chord formula: 1 ♭3 ♭5 ♭7)

A minor 7th flat 5th chord is labeled with the suffix "m7♭5" and consists of a diminished chord with an added minor 7th. Another name for this chord is "half diminished," designated with the suffix "ø." With either name, it is the same chord. Below are five different m7♭5 forms, which correspond to the five different forms established on page 58. To play specific letter-named chords with these forms, position the root on the correct note.

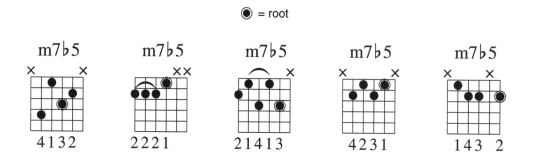

Augmented (chord formula: 1 3 #5)

An augmented chord is labeled with the suffix "aug" or the symbol "+" and consists of a major chord with a raised, or sharped 5th tone. Below are five different augmented forms, which corresond to the five different forms established on page 58. In addition, each of these forms may be shifted up or down the neck in four-fret intervals, creating different inversions of the same augmented chord. To play specific letter-named chords with these forms, position the root on the correct note.

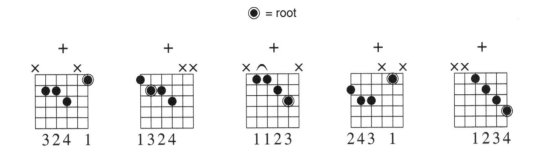

Augmented 7th (chord formula: 1 3 #5 ♭7)

An augmented 7th chord is labeled with the suffix "aug7" or "+7" and consists of an augmented chord with an added minor 7th tone. Below are five different augmented 7th forms, which correspond to the five different forms established on page 58. To play specific letter-named chords with these forms, position the root on the correct note.

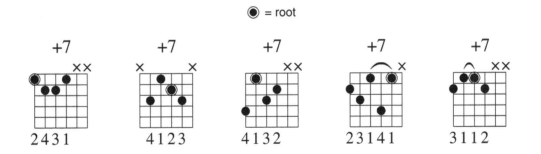

Augmented 7th flat 9th (chord formula: 1 3 #5 ♭7 ♭9)

An augmented 7th flat 9th chord is labeled with the suffix "+7♭9" and consists of an augmented 7th chord with an added ♭9th tone. Below are five different +7♭9 forms, which roughly correspond to the five different forms established on page 58. To play specific letter-named chords with these forms, position the root on the correct note.

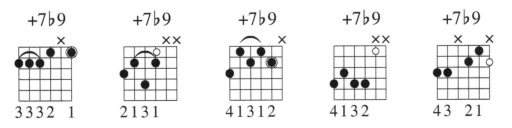

7th flat 5th (chord formula: 1 3 ♭5 ♭7)

A 7th flat 5th chord is labeled with the suffix "7♭5" and consists of a dominant 7th chord with a lowered 5th tone. These four forms correspond to the first four forms established on page 58. To play specific letter-named chords with these forms, position the root on the correct note.

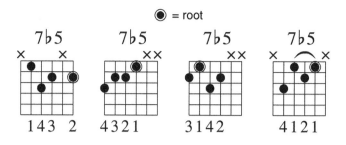

7th flat 9th (chord formula: 1 3 5 ♭7 ♭9)

A 7th flat 9th chord is labeled with the suffix "7♭9" and consists of a dominant 7th chord with an added ♭9th tone. These four forms correspond to the first four forms established on page 58. To play specific letter-named chords with these forms, position the root on the correct note.

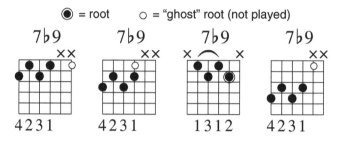

7th sharp 9th (chord formula: 1 3 5 ♭7 ♯9)

A 7th sharp 9th chord is labeled with the suffix "7♯9" and consists of a dominant 7th chord with an added ♯9th tone. These four forms correspond to the first four forms established on page 58. To play specific letter-named chords with these forms, position the root on the correct note.

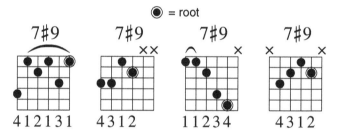

6th (chord formula: 1 3 5 6)
6th added 9th (chord formula: 1 3 5 6 9)
Minor 6th (chord formula: 1 ♭3 5 6)

A 6th chord is labeled with the suffix "6" and consists of a major chord with an added 6th tone. The two 6th chord forms shown here correspond to the first and fourth forms on page 58. A 6th added 9th chord simply adds the 9th tone. The two forms here correspond to the first and third forms on page 58. A minor 6th is a minor chord with an added 6th tone. The two minor 6th forms correspond to the first and fourth forms on page 58. To play specific letter-name chords with these forms, position the root on the correct note.

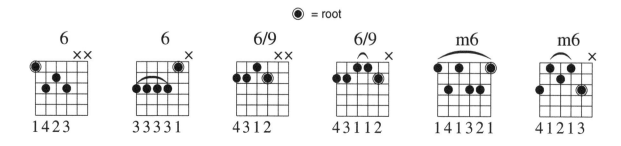

Scale Reference

Scales are groups of notes used in music and arranged into a specific sequence or structure. This section is a reference for constructing, locating, and playing the essential scales in several different positions and formats.

First, each scale is shown on the staff based upon the root note C. The numerical formula that is commonly used to describe the scale (in any key) is also shown, along with its specific interval pattern. Then the scale is shown in three formats: laid out on a single string, in position patterns, and in diagonal patterns. All are *movable patterns*.

Using movable scale patterns

As with the chord shapes in the previous section, each scale pattern shown here may be shifted up or down the neck to play in any key (based on any root note). Use the neck diagram below if you need to find the correct position for any specific root note.

- First, the scale is shown on a **single string**. To play it in another key, simply slide the whole sequence up or down the neck to place the pattern's root on the root note that you want. It can also be moved and played on any of the six strings of the guitar. This is useful for practicing as it helps you learn the intervallic structure of the scale.

- Next, the **position patterns** show all available notes of each scale type in two different positions. The first position begins with its root on the sixth string. This may also be referred to as the "primary" position and can be associated with the E-form chord shape shown on page 58. The second position pattern has its root on the fifth string. This may be called the "secondary" position and can be associated with the A-form chord shape. Again, simply match one of the root notes to its respective note on the fingerboard. The rest of the pattern follows accordingly.

- Finally, the **diagonal patterns** show another common way that this scale-type can appear. In the case of a diatonic (seven-tone) scale, this will be a three-note-per-string pattern. Move these to any key in the same way as the previous patterns.

The notes on the neck are shown below. Above fret 12, the pattern of notes repeats an octave higher. So fret 13 is the same as fret 1 (up an octave), fret 14 is the same as fret 2 (up an octave), etc. Use these note names to find the correct root positions for the following scales.

E	Eb/D#	D	Db/C#	C	B	Bb/A#	A	Ab/G#	G	Gb/F#	F	E
B	Bb/A#	A	Ab/G#	G	Gb/F#	F	E	Eb/D#	D	Db/C#	C	B
G	Gb/F#	F	E	Eb/D#	D	Db/C#	C	B	Bb/A#	A	Ab/G#	G
D	Db/C#	C	B	Bb/A#	A	Ab/G#	G	Gb/F#	F	E	Eb/D#	D
A	Ab/G#	G	Gb/F#	F	E	Eb/D#	D	Db/C#	C	B	Bb/A#	A
E	Eb/D#	D	Db/C#	C	B	Bb/A#	A	Ab/G#	G	Gb/F#	F	E

12   9   7   5   3

Major

The most common scale in Western music is the major scale. It consists of seven different tones (diatonic). Practice it both ascending and descending in various keys.

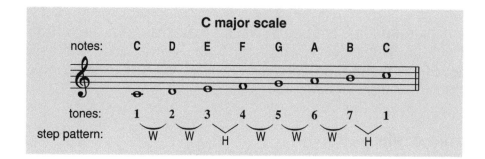

On one string:

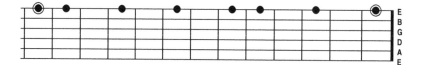

Position patterns:

Primary (E-form)   Secondary (A-form)

Diagonal patterns:

Primary—three notes per string

Secondary—three notes per string

Minor

The natural minor scale, also called "pure minor" or the "Aeolian mode," is used in nearly all styles of Western music. It is also a diatonic scale. Practice it both ascending and descending in various keys.

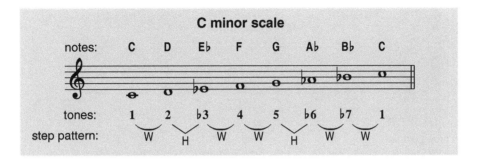

On one string:

Position patterns:

Primary (E-form)   Secondary (A-form)

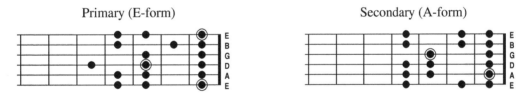

Diagonal patterns:

Primary—three notes per string

Secondary—three notes per string

Harmonic Minor

The harmonic minor scale is an altered version of the natural minor scale. It is common in classical music. It is also a diatonic scale, consisting of seven different tones. Practice both ascending and descending in various keys.

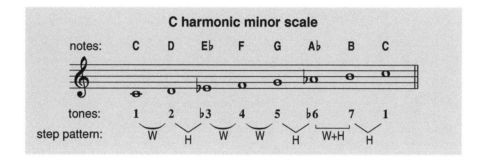

On one string:

Position patterns:

Primary (E-form)

Secondary (A-form)

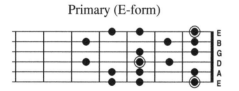
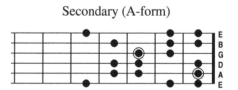

Diagonal patterns:

Primary—three notes per string

Secondary—three notes per string

Melodic Minor

This scale is also known as the "jazz minor" scale. It blends elements of the major scale (in the upper notes) with a minor scale's lower portion. Practice both ascending and descending in various keys.

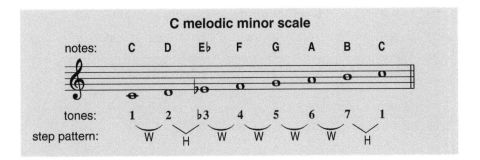

On one string:

Position patterns:

Primary (E-form)   Secondary (A-form)

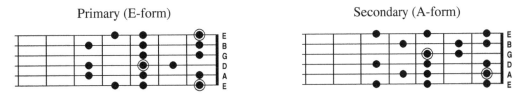

Diagonal patterns:

Primary—three notes per string

Secondary—three notes per string

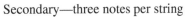

Minor Pentatonic

This is the most common scale in rock and blues. As its name suggests ("penta" means five), this scale is a minor scale with only five tones, as as opposed to the previous diatonic, or seven-tone, scales. Practice both ascending and descending in various keys.

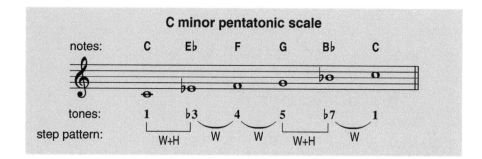

On one string:

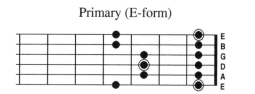

Position patterns:

Primary (E-form)   Secondary (A-form)

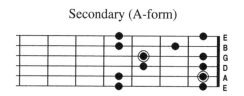

Diagonal patterns:

Primary—with low and high extensions

Secondary—with low and high extensions

Major Pentatonic

This is another five-tone scale used in many styles of music. It has a bright quality that lends itself to country and major-key rock styles. Practice both ascending and descending in various keys.

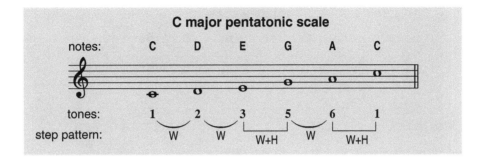

On one string:

Position patterns:

Primary (E-form)   Secondary (A-form)

Diagonal patterns:

Primary—with low and high extensions

Secondary—with low and high extensions

Blues

The blues scale is common in rock, jazz, and of course, blues. It is similar to the minor pentatonic, but with an added ♭5 "blues" tone. Practice both ascending and descending in various keys.

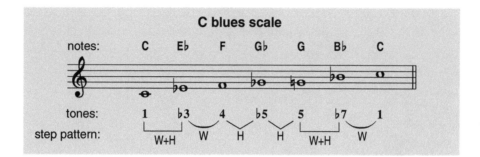

On one string:

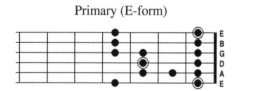

Position patterns:

Primary (E-form)

Secondary (A-form)

Diagonal patterns:

Primary—with low and high extensions

Secondary—with low and high extensions

Diminished

This scale is popular in jazz and metal styles. It is an eight-tone-per-octave, or "octatonic" scale, composed of alternating whole and half steps. For this reason, it is also sometimes called the "whole-half" scale. Practice ascending and descending in various keys.

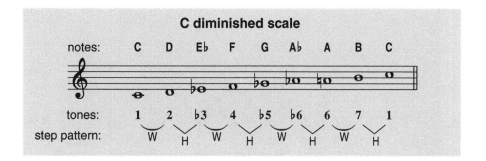

On one string:

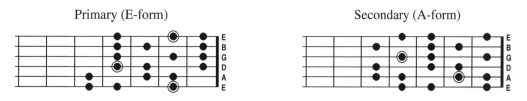

Position patterns:

Primary (E-form)   Secondary (A-form)

Diagonal patterns:

Primary—four notes per string

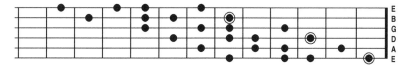

Secondary—four notes per string

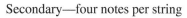
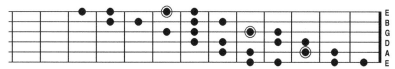

Modes

Modes are scales derived from another scale by displacing the root note. If we take the C major scale, for example, and play it from D to D, and now regard the note D as the root (but still using the notes of C major), we have the *second mode* of the major scale. The *third mode* of C major would begin on the third tone (E) of the scale, and so on. All the modes of C major are shown below. Each mode can function like a scale in its own right—with its own interval sequence and tonal structure.

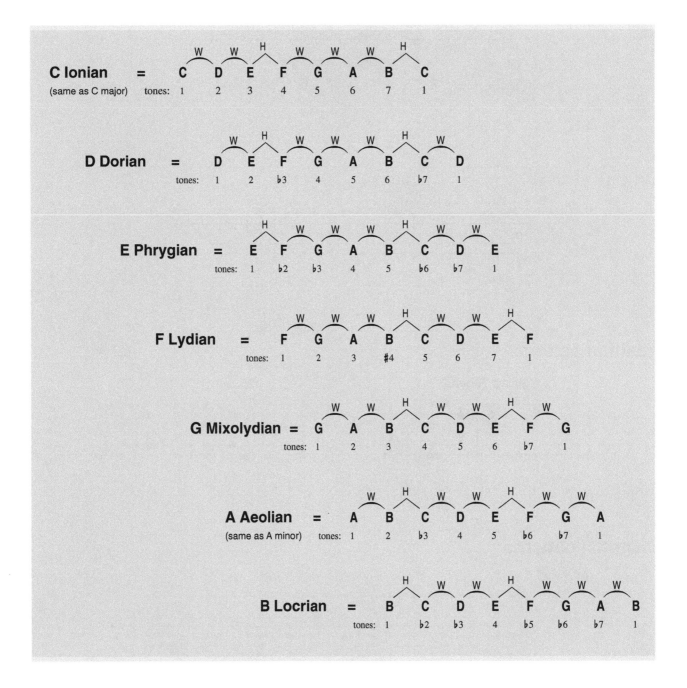

The next page shows the primary (E-form) and secondary (A-form) position patterns for each of the modes of the major scale. Play each ascending and descending in various keys, just like the previous scales.

Primary (E-forms)	Secondary (A-forms)

Ionian
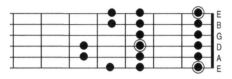

Dorian
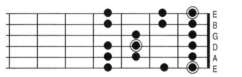

Phrygian
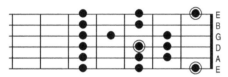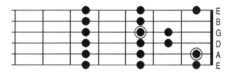

Lydian
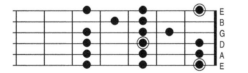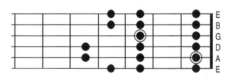

Mixolydian
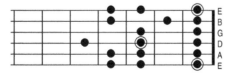

Aeolian
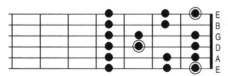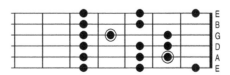

Locrian

Using Right-Handed Materials

The vast majority of learning material for guitar is written from a right-handed perspective. Therefore, it is a good idea to become well-versed in reading right-handed chord boxes and neck diagrams. This isn't extraordinarily difficult, but it does take a little getting used to.

Basically, every chord box you see will be the mirror image of those you have learned in this book. Notice the relationship below.

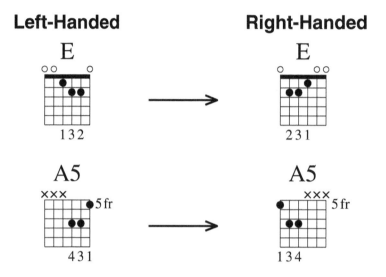

An easy way to translate is to imagine that your guitar neck is transparent and you are looking at the right-handed chord shape *through the back of the neck.* With a little practice, this will become second nature. (In fact, this author is actually right-handed and used this method to translate all chord boxes into their left-handed versions. So I can guarantee it works!) Another option is to imagine that the page is a *mirror*—the right-handed chord boxes are literally a *reflection* of what your left hand should be playing. (Try this in front of a mirror, and you'll see what I mean.)

Finally, you'll also need to get used to seeing neck diagrams in reverse. The "through the back of the neck" approach doesn't work here, but the good news is that this translation is easier and less confusing than dealing with chord boxes. Study the neck diagrams below and notice the mirror-image effect.

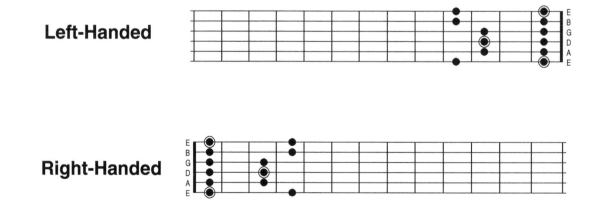

Get Better at Guitar

...with these Great Guitar Instruction Books from Hal Leonard!

101 GUITAR TIPS
INCLUDES TAB

STUFF ALL THE PROS KNOW AND USE

by Adam St. James

This book contains invaluable guidance on everything from scales and music theory to truss rod adjustments, proper recording studio set-ups, and much more.

00695737 Book/Online Audio $16.99

AMAZING PHRASING
INCLUDES TAB

by Tom Kolb

This book/audio pack explores all the main components necessary for crafting well-balanced rhythmic and melodic phrases. It also explains how these phrases are put together to form cohesive solos. The companion audio contains 89 demo tracks, most with full-band backing.

00695583 Book/Online Audio $19.99

ARPEGGIOS FOR THE MODERN GUITARIST
INCLUDES TAB

by Tom Kolb

Using this no-nonsense book with online audio, guitarists will learn to apply and execute all types of arpeggio forms using a variety of techniques, including alternate picking, sweep picking, tapping, string skipping, and legato.

00695862 Book/Online Audio $19.99

BLUES YOU CAN USE

by John Ganapes

This comprehensive source for learning blues guitar is designed to develop both your lead and rhythm playing. Includes: 21 complete solos • blues chords, progressions and riffs • turnarounds • movable scales and soloing techniques • string bending • utilizing the entire fingerboard • and more.

00142420 Book/Online Media..................................$19.99

CONNECTING PENTATONIC PATTERNS
INCLUDES TAB

by Tom Kolb

If you've been finding yourself trapped in the pentatonic box, this book is for you! This hands-on book with online audio offers examples for guitar players of all levels, from beginner to advanced. Study this book faithfully, and soon you'll be soloing all over the neck with the greatest of ease.

00696445 Book/Online Audio $19.99

FRETBOARD MASTERY
INCLUDES TAB

by Troy Stetina

Untangle the mysterious regions of the guitar fretboard and unlock your potential. This book familiarizes you with all the shapes you need to know by applying them in real musical examples, thereby reinforcing and reaffirming your newfound knowledge.

00695331 Book/Online Audio $19.99

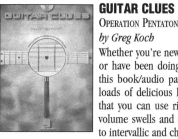

GUITAR AEROBICS
INCLUDES TAB

by Troy Nelson

Here is a daily dose of guitar "vitamins" to keep your chops fine tuned! Musical styles include rock, blues, jazz, metal, country, and funk. Techniques taught include alternate picking, arpeggios, sweep picking, string skipping, legato, string bending, and rhythm guitar.

00695946 Book/Online Audio $19.99

GUITAR CLUES
INCLUDES TAB

OPERATION PENTATONIC

by Greg Koch

Whether you're new to improvising or have been doing it for a while, this book/audio pack will provide loads of delicious licks and tricks that you can use right away, from volume swells and chicken pickin' to intervallic and chordal ideas.

00695827 Book/Online Audio $19.99

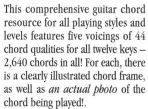

PAT METHENY – GUITAR ETUDES
INCLUDES TAB

Over the years, in many master classes and workshops around the world, Pat has demonstrated the kind of daily workout he puts himself through. This book includes a collection of 14 guitar etudes he created to help you limber up, improve picking technique and build finger independence.

00696587..$15.99

PICTURE CHORD ENCYCLOPEDIA

This comprehensive guitar chord resource for all playing styles and levels features five voicings of 44 chord qualities for all twelve keys – 2,640 chords in all! For each, there is a clearly illustrated chord frame, as well as *an actual photo* of the chord being played!.

00695224..$19.99

RHYTHM GUITAR 365
INCLUDES TAB

by Troy Nelson

This book provides 365 exercises – one for every day of the year! – to keep your rhythm chops fine tuned. Topics covered include: chord theory; the fundamentals of rhythm; fingerpicking; strum patterns; diatonic and non-diatonic progressions; triads; major and minor keys; and more.

00103627 Book/Online Audio $24.99

SCALE CHORD RELATIONSHIPS
INCLUDES TAB

by Michael Mueller & Jeff Schroedl

This book/audio pack explains how to: recognize keys • analyze chord progressions • use the modes • play over nondiatonic harmony • use harmonic and melodic minor scales • use symmetrical scales • incorporate exotic scales • and much more!

00695563 Book/Online Audio $14.99

SPEED MECHANICS FOR LEAD GUITAR
INCLUDES TAB

by Troy Stetina

Take your playing to the stratosphere with this advanced lead book which will help you develop speed and precision in today's explosive playing styles. Learn the fastest ways to achieve speed and control, secrets to make your practice time really count, and how to open your ears and make your musical ideas more solid and tangible.

00699323 Book/Online Audio $19.99

TOTAL ROCK GUITAR
INCLUDES TAB

by Troy Stetina

This comprehensive source for learning rock guitar is designed to develop both lead and rhythm playing. It covers: getting a tone that rocks • open chords, power chords and barre chords • riffs, scales and licks • string bending, strumming, and harmonics • and more.

00695246 Book/Online Audio $19.99

Guitar World Presents
STEVE VAI'S GUITAR WORKOUT
INCLUDES TAB

In this book, Steve Vai reveals his path to virtuoso enlightenment with two challenging guitar workouts – one 10-hour and one 30-hour – which include scale and chord exercises, ear training, sight-reading, music theory, and much more.

00119643..$14.99